Lexington Historical Society

Proceedings of Lexington Historical Society and Papers Relating to the History of the Town

Vol. III

Lexington Historical Society

Proceedings of Lexington Historical Society and Papers Relating to the History of the Town
Vol. III

ISBN/EAN: 9783337221300

Printed in Europe, USA, Canada, Australia, Japan

Cover: Foto ©ninafisch / pixelio.de

More available books at **www.hansebooks.com**

PROCEEDINGS

OF THE

LEXINGTON HISTORICAL SOCIETY

AND PAPERS RELATING TO THE

HISTORY OF THE TOWN

PRESENTED AT SOME OF ITS MEETINGS.

VOL. III.

LEXINGTON, MASSACHUSETTS
PUBLISHED BY THE LEXINGTON HISTORICAL SOCIETY
1905

CONTENTS.

	PAGE.
SKETCH OF LIFE OF HON. THOMAS HANCOCK	5
DR. STILLMAN SPAULDING	19
THE PARISH OF CAMBRIDGE FARMS	25
CHARLES FOLLEN	42
ORIGIN OF THE LEXINGTON AND WEST CAMBRIDGE BRANCH RAILROAD	58
SOME MEMORIES OF THE LEXINGTON CENTENNIAL	62
RECOLLECTIONS OF THE THIRD MEETING-HOUSE	82
THE EPITAPHS IN THE BURYING-GROUNDS	95
THE CONCORD TURNPIKE	110
EARLY DAYS OF THE HIGH SCHOOL	117
CLOCK-MAKING IN LEXINGTON	134
HOW THE HANCOCK-CLARKE HOUSE WAS SAVED	138
THE MUNROE TAVERN	142
MR. CHARLES A. WELLINGTON	155
MR. GEORGE O. SMITH	164
REV. CARLTON A. STAPLES	177
PROCEEDINGS	i. to xi.
GIFTS	xii. to xvii.
MEMBERSHIP	xix. and xx.
NECROLOGY	xxi. and xxii.
INDEX	xxiii. to xxvi.

A SKETCH OF THE LIFE OF HON. THOMAS HANCOCK, A NATIVE OF LEXINGTON.

READ BY REV. C. A. STAPLES, MARCH 8, 1887.

Among Hogarth's pictures, designed to teach certain great moral lessons, there is a series entitled "The Industrious and the Idle Apprentice." In these he represents the course of two young men apprenticed to a silk weaver in London, a hundred and fifty years ago. In the first plate we have the young men working at their looms. The industrious apprentice appears cheerful and happy, intent upon his work and trying to accomplish as much as possible. Beside him lies an open book which he is supposed to be reading whenever his eyes can be safely withdrawn from his work — a book of an instructive and moral character. His appearance is that of a tidy, self-respecting, open-hearted fellow, determined to make his way in the world through his own work and worth. The other, the idler, is represented as yawning over his work, from the effects of the last night's debauch, sullen and repulsive in countenance, with copies of ribald songs hung up around him, which he is evidently learning, and with a huge pot of beer standing hard by. His appearance is slovenly and coarse; he seems careless in his work, and only concerned to get through with it as easily as possible, that he may be ready for another night of dissipation and folly.

The second plate represents the way in which they spend Sunday. The industrious apprentice is seen in the congregation at Church, joining in the service of worship with his master's daughter who holds the hymn book with him from which they are singing together with evident satisfaction and delight. The idler has stolen away from Church into the adjoining burying ground, where with his associates he is engaged in gambling, using a horizontal tombstone for a table while the sexton, who has discovered them, is about to cudgel them over the head with his cane.

In the fourth plate we have the industrious apprentice advanced from the weaver's stall to the counting room, where he keeps the books, and holds the keys of his master's purse, while the idle fellow is driven out of the shop and sent off to sea for vicious courses.

The next scene introduces us to a wedding with its festivities and rejoicing, where the industrious apprentice marries his master's daughter, and becomes his partner in business, while the idle one, returning from sea, becomes the associate of vile creatures, who live in wretched garrets and support themselves by thieving.

In the next our industrious and prosperous young man becomes an Alderman of London, and as one of the magistrates of the city, his former fellow apprentice is brought before him to be tried for murder. And the series closes with the Alderman, become Lord Mayor, and in his splendid coach, when riding to his inauguration in Guild Hall, he passes his old associate on his way to the scaffold to die for his crimes.

Thus industry, morality and religion lead to promotion, wealth and honor; while idleness, dissipation and folly lead to poverty, suffering and shame. Such are the lessons which these pictures forcibly, characteristically and happily teach. They are a series of sermons illustrating great principles of human conduct preached in pictures rather than words.

No doubt Hogarth drew both characters from the life

which he saw around him in the London shops and streets. But he certainly could have found in Boston, living at the very time his pictures were made, a man who almost exactly answered to his delineation of the fortunes of the industrious apprentice. I mean Thomas Hancock, the son of Rev. John Hancock, the second minister of Lexington.

The old Hancock House on Hancock Street, in Lexington has a small gambrel roofed ell, one story in height and in dimension 24 ft. by 21. It constitutes the original house built by the minister in 1698, when he was ordained and settled over what was then the parish of Cambridge Farms. In one of the two attic chambers of this humble dwelling, Thomas Hancock, the second son of the minister, was born July 13th, 1703, and five days afterwards, Sunday, July 18, as the Church records show, he was taken to the meeting house and baptized by his father. Thus early in life he was inducted into the way of religious observances.

His education was probably conducted by his father and consisted of little more than a knowledge of the three Rs. At that time there was no school in the parish, so far as we know, and the minister was, not unlikely, the only person capable of teaching the common English branches and preparing young men for college. Parson Hancock sent two of his sons, John and Ebenezer, to Harvard, for which they were prepared by his own instruction. It used to be said that whenever a New England family had a boy who was not good to work, he was sent to college, and made into a minister. However this may have been with the Hancock sons, it is certain that Thomas was a good boy to work and that he was not sent to college, while his older and younger brothers were in due time made into ministers.

Imagine the boy at fourteen trudging along the highway, with his stock of clothing tied up in a handkerchief and slung over his shoulder upon a stick, his only worldly possessions, making his way to Boston, where he was apprenticed in 1718 to Samuel Gerrish and Sarah, his wife, a bookbinder and stationer. He was a bright, quick-witted, wide-awake lad and soon gave promise of higher things than book-binding and book-selling, though he served out his apprenticeship and learned the business thoroughly. No sooner had he completed his term of service, probably in 1725, than we find him setting up for himself in the same trade, possibly with the assistance of his master, or perhaps taking the business of Gerrish into his hands, while his master retired. Certain it is that he was soon established in a store of his own on Ann Street, called "Stationer's Arms," where he secured a large and prosperous trade and where he remained for many years. Here the latest books of Theology, Law, Medicine, Science, Religion and other departments of literature were to be found imported from Longman's in London, or published in America. He seems to have risen rapidly in wealth, social position and influence. Probably he soon embarked in larger enterprises than bookbinding and selling.

We find him engaged in the retail dry goods business, and the selectmen of Lexington entered in their accounts with the town bills of such articles as mourning gloves bought, I suppose, for the funerals of paupers, at the store of Thomas Hancock. It is certain that he became a large shipping merchant, trading with various foreign countries, sending out cargoes of dried fish, corn and tobacco, and bringing home wine and fruit, sugar and silks.

But in the meantime he had taken to himself a wife, in the person of Lydia Henchman. He had not been an industrious and faithful apprentice in vain, nor a constant attendant upon the Sunday services of Brattle Street Church, where the Henchmans worshipped, without winning the confidence of the family and making a favorable impression upon the heart of the daughter. And so his marriage with the fair Lydia, who is said to have been a beautiful girl, was consummated and a close alliance with one of the most prominent and respectable families of the Church and the town. The Henchman mansion was in Court Street, on the site of what was till recently the Adams Express Company's building, that huge, iron front edifice, standing on the south side a little below Tremont Street. It came into the possession of Mrs. Hancock from her father's estate, and was given by her to Brattle Street Church, after the death of her husband, for a parsonage. Here the ministers of that Church, Dr. Cooper, Buckminster, Edward Everett, Dr. Palfrey and Dr. Lothrop resided, until within 40 years, when it was sold and a new parsonage on Chestnut Street bought. Here died that great preacher, Joseph Stevens Buckminster, whose Church was so thronged, that as I once heard an old lady say, who in her childhood used to go there with her parents, ladders were sometimes placed against the walls on the outside, and at the windows, and when all the space inside was filled, people climbed up and sat on the window sills, listening to the silver tones of Buckminster's eloquence.

In the year 1735, Thomas Hancock, then but 32 years old, had accumulated money enough to justify him in taking steps to build a house for his future home. He accordingly bought the land on the south side of Beacon Hill, including the present site of the State House and extending some distance to the west of it and from the Common back over the hill to Derne Street, including a portion of what was known as the reservoir lot, embracing 6½ acres of the most desirable ground for residence in Boston. He began building his house in the following year, and it was completed and occupied by him in 1737.

All who were familiar with the Boston of 40 years ago, readily recall the appearance of the old Hancock mansion, standing a little west of the State House, and some distance back from Beacon Street, fronting the Common — a substantial structure of stone, two stories in height, with the front door in the centre, and a portico supported by handsome fluted columns, with carved capitals. There were two windows upon each side of the door, in the front of the lower story, and five windows in the upper story. The roof was of the style common in that day, called "gambrel," with three dormer windows and with a balustrade at the peak, running the whole length and enclosing a considerable space where the family could go out for an airing, and obtain an extensive view over the city, the harbor and the surrounding country. The house was approached from the street by broad stone steps, through a yard laid out in two or more terraces and planted with choice shrubs and flowers. Originally, there was an ell containing a spacious dining room on the east side, extending towards the State House, and a similar ell on the west end, containing the servants' rooms, and extending back to the stables, in the rear, behind the house; but these had disappeared before my remembrance. Rising up the slope of Beacon Hill, where Mt. Vernon and Pinckney Streets are now, were extensive fruit, flower and vegetable gardens, crowned with a summer house from which opened a wide prospect over the land and the sea; and where the State House now stands, was Hancock's cow-pasture.

The interior of the house was divided above and below by a wide hall running through it, from front to rear. The rooms were spacious and elegant, finished with elaborate carvings, in the style of that day, and hung with rich and curious papers. Everything without and within this lordly mansion gave evidence of a taste for substantial and beautiful things, and an ample fortune to gratify the taste. The owner was evidently a prosperous and wealthy man, who took delight in well-kept grounds, a fine equipage and a generous hospitality, who used his money freely wherever it brought him comfort, luxury and social distinction.

Thus we find the Lexington apprentice boy, after 25 years of hard work, wise planning and careful saving, the owner of the finest house and estate in Boston. He had risen by the force of character, from the bindery to the counting room, and from the counting room to the head of the establishment, to become its director and owner. The industrious apprentice was thought good enough even to possess the hand of Lydia Henchman, and he took her from the plain house of her father in Court Street, and made her mistress of a splendid mansion on Beacon Hill; too far away from the centre of business, in a bleak and lonely spot, it was said, but all confessed that it was a beautiful situation when once they reached it. In one of his letters to a friend he says, "We are living very comfortably in our house on Beacon Hill." But it was a long time, I suppose, before there were any neighbors nearer than old Peter Faneuil, the great merchant, whose house stood nearly opposite King's Chapel on Tremont Street, and whom Thomas Hancock speaks of in one of his letters as "The toppinist man in Boston."

In the Boston Public Library, there is a great mass of manuscript letters, account books, and other papers that belonged to Thomas Hancock, which were found in the old Hancock mansion, when it was torn down in 1863. Here are the contracts for building the grand house, drawn up in his hand-writing, and copies of his business letters to his correspondents in England, ordering materials for the house and its furnishings — the flowers, shrubs and trees for his grounds, and books and merchandise for his store. Some of them are very curious and interesting and they reveal strikingly the habits and the character of the man; his careful, methodical, pains-taking business methods; his anxiety to keep all the trade in his line of business in his own hands and crowd out every competitor; his sharp, shrewd way of dealing with the London merchants to bring his goods down to the lowest figure. He evidently followed the advice of one of the Rothchilds, "To be successful you must buy sheep and sell deer." When ordering books, for instance, he would write that he wanted a particular one for his own use and wished the binding to be especially handsome, and suggested in view of the fact that his trade was very considerable with them, whether they would not be pleased to make him a present of it. He never hesitates to tell precisely what he wants — there are no sly hints, no circumlocution in presenting the matter — he puts it in words that leave no chance for misunderstanding. He wants the best at the lowest price, and if something nice be thrown in to adorn the garden or the house, so much the better. In planting his grounds with trees, shrubs and flowers he had great tribulation. They were ordered from London, and they were to be rare, choice and beautiful. But hardly anything lived which he received. The trees would not grow; the seeds never sprouted; many pounds in value proved a total loss and he writes to the nursery-man in England complaining bitterly, "If you are an honest man," he says, "you will replace this order with a new lot that are sound and good, without cost. Even those things which you sent me as a present, were all worthless You cannot expect to extend your trade here unless you make this loss good." Thus a hundred and fifty years ago we find that all the seed sold was not sound and all the trees planted did not grow, and buyers then were like the buyers now, aye, like buyers 3000 years ago, in the time of Solomon, who tells us that they used to cry " It is nought, it is nought," and then go their way and boast of their good bargains. In ordering his paper-hanging, he wants a particular pattern, which he has seen in the house of a friend, full of peacocks, mocking-birds, monkeys, squirrels, fruits and flowers, but if possible, handsomer, as he says, " with more birds flying about in the air and with a landskip at the bottom."

Among the Hancock papers was found a curious letter of Peter Faneuil's to an agent of his in the West Indies, advising him of the shipment of a quantity of dried fish which he is directed to sell for his advantage and invest the proceeds in a straight-limbed negro boy, 12 or 15 years old, one who has had the small-pox, and is of a tractable disposition. Thus the great merchant whom Hancock calls the "toppinist" man in Boston, exchanged codfish for negroes. He gave Faneuil Hall, which became the cradle of Liberty, to the town of Boston. And within that hall were held the great meetings, which did much to arouse public sentiment against slavery and destroy the institution that Faneuil upheld by precept and example.

We find Thomas Hancock, the Lexington apprentice boy, prosperous and wealthy, settled in his Beacon Hill mansion in 1737. His rooms are adorned with those wonderful paper-hangings, and his gardens planted with all rare and beautiful things brought from England, which he was coaxing to grow. For twenty-seven years he lived there, dispensing a generous hospitality and drawing around him the leading people of Boston, in social standing and influence. He still continued his book and dry goods store, but a much larger and more profitable business was his trade with foreign countries. This was probably the principal source of his great fortune, which rose from the contents of the handkerchief brought to Boston, to be the largest fortune in New England. He invested his money extensively in lands. In some of the country towns of Massachusetts he was an extensive owner of real estate, and in the district of Maine, then belonging to Massachusetts, he owned whole townships and counties amounting, I think, to more than 100,000 acres. But he was not simply a sagacious, enterprising, successful merchant and trader, but a kindhearted son and brother, and a compassionate and liberal man in his relations to the poor and suffering.

When he was building the great mansion on Beacon Hill in 1735 and 1736 for himself, he was also making a large addition to his father's house in Lexington, and doing much to make the last days of the old folks comfortable and happy. The two-story portion of the house fronting the south, and finished in large and handsome rooms, was erected at the same time as the stone mansion in Boston.

His older brother John, the minister of Braintree, and his younger brother, Ebenezer, colleague pastor, with his father, of the Church in Lexington, both died in early manhood, leaving dependent families. Thomas Hancock had no children of his own but he seems to have exercised a paternal care over those of his deceased brothers educating them and providing handsomely for them in his will. John Hancock, who became President of the Continental Congress and first Governor of Massachusetts, under the new Constitution, was the son of his brother John, minister of Braintree, and was his favorite nephew. He educated him at Harvard, took him into his counting room, after graduation, sent him to England on business, where he witnessed the coronation of George III, and left him an estate of more than half a million dollars. This wealth inherited from his uncle, and which he did nothing to increase, but rather depleted, gave Governor John Hancock a high social position and his great prominence among the patriots in the opening scenes of the Revolution. Thus the Lexington apprentice boy perhaps did as much to make John Hancock what he was, as any superior ability or merit of his own.

But few rich men were on the patriot side. The wealth, aristocracy and social distinction belonged mainly to the Tories. That a young man of fine accomplishments and aristocratic connections, having the second largest fortune in the country, for probably it was the largest next to Washington's, had enlisted in the patriot cause, was of immense consequence to that cause and naturally secured for him great consideration and enabled him to render grand service in the struggle for National independence. Thomas Hancock was an active man in charitable, religious and political affairs. It is said that he was fond of the clergy, as good men usually are, and delighted to receive and entertain them at his spacious mansion.

We learn from his order books that his cellar was well stocked with the choicest wines and liquors, and the best foreign fruits, and that his table was adorned with the choicest glass, china and silver-ware that the London shops afforded and was supplied with the most toothsome edibles in the Boston markets. And if he really did have great fondness for the clergy, it is no wonder that the clergy were fond of him, and were frequently found eating at his hospitable board and sleeping in his prophet's chamber. In his will he leaves £200 in money and a mourning suit to his beloved pastor, Dr. Cooper, and bequests to four other clergymen, including Jonas Clark of Lexington, who married his niece, Lucy Bowes. Naturally enough the clergy of that day may have thought that "of such is the kingdom of Heaven!" But his charities were much broader than this. The first number of Hunt's Merchants' Magazine contains a notice of Thomas Hancock which speaks of his sympathy with the suffering of all classes and conditions. It tells us that the poor were never turned away from his door unfed and that no cause of education, philanthropy or of religion was denied his help and his bounty.

It is a striking fact also that he leaves a bequest of £1000 to Boston for the care of the insane poor. In his will made 150 years ago when little or nothing had been done for these sad wrecks of humanity, often chained up for years in rags and filth and left to die like beasts, Thomas Hancock remembered their miserable condition and devoted five thousand dollars of his fortune to their alleviation and comfort. It shows that a good heart beat in his bosom; he felt that he owed something to these poor and wretched creatures out of the wealth with which his life had been crowned. A professorship of Hebrew was founded in Harvard College by a bequest in his will, and £1000 given to the Society for propagating the Gospel among the Indians. Bequests were also made to the poor of Brattle Street Church, and a sum of money to the Church in Lexington, to procure two communion cups as memorials of his interest and affection. His brothers' and sisters' children were liberally remembered in gifts of money or lands, while the mansion on Beacon Hill with its furniture, plate, pictures and books and with his horses and carriages, was left to his wife and £10,000 sterling in money, the mansion to go to his nephew, John, after her death, with the residue of his estate.

During the last years of his life he was elected a member of the Governor's Council. In connection with the French and Indian Wars, he rendered important service to the Colony and the English Government in fitting out various expeditions against the enemy. He was a man of sound judgment, of inflexible honesty, of broad, enterprising spirit; keen and sagacious in the pursuit of money but liberal in using it; warm and true in friendship, given to hospitality, faithful to his convictions and firm in his religious principles and habits, a man who, like thousands of New England boys born in humble country homes, by the sheer force of a sound and sturdy character, made his way from poverty to affluence, and become a power for good in the community and the State.

At noon, August 1st, 1764, just as he was entering the door of the Council Chamber, in the old State House, he was attacked with apoplexy and fell insensible upon the floor. He was removed to his own house, where he lingered for a few hours in an unconscious state and peacefully passed away in the 62nd year of his age. The dark clouds soon to break in the thunder and tempest of the Revolution were beginning to gather thick and fast in the political heavens. The mutterings of the coming storm were plainly heard; but he was happily spared the sight of the devastation and misery which it caused here. And he was spared what would not unlikely have been a severer trial, the choice which he would have been compelled to make between the cause of the king and that of the people. It was left for his nephew, John Hancock, probably a man inferior to him in strength and excellence of character, to make the choice and to attain the prominence and the fame which have been awarded him in history, but which the good name and the great fortune of Thomas Hancock opened to him and made possible for him. His widow, Lydia Henchman Hancock, survived her husband above 11 years, occupying the famous mansion, and with her nephew John maintaining a large and generous hospitality. She was a near relative of the Quincy family and seems to have exercised guardian care over Dorothy Quincy, daughter of Edmund, a noted Boston merchant, whom John Hancock married at Fairfield, Conn., Sept. 4th, 1775.

The following inscription is taken from the tombstone at the grave of Madam Thomas Hancock, in the old burying ground at Fairfield:

> THIS STONE ERECTED
> BY THADDEUS BURR AND EUNICE BURR
> TO THE MEMORY OF THEIR DEAR FRIEND
> MRS. LYDIA HANCOCK,
> RELICT OF THE HON[BLE] THOS. HANCOCK, ESQR.
> OF BOSTON,
> Whose Remains lie here interred, having retired to this town from
> the calamities of war, during the Blockade of her native
> city in 1775. Just on her return to the reenjoy-
> ment of an ample fortune.
> On April 15th A. D. 1776
> She was seized with apoplexy and closed a life of
> unaffected piety, universal benevolence
> and extensive charity.

DR. STILLMAN SPAULDING.

READ BY RALPH E. LANE, MARCH 11, 1890.

Of the men once prominent in Lexington none is more gratefully remembered by his townspeople than Dr. Stillman Spaulding. Although not numbered among its earliest inhabitants, the Spaulding family has been identified with this town for many years. Those who knew its originator here in the days when he ministered to them as their physician and friend, will recall many acts which endeared him in so remarkable a degree to the hearts of his neighbors.

Entering upon the practice of medicine in this town in the early part of the last century, the immediate successor of Dr. Joseph Fisk, he exemplified that nobility of character which is the delight of all good men.

Dr. Spaulding was born in Chelmsford, Mass., Aug 17, 1788. His father was Job Spaulding and his mother Sarah Proctor. From this union resulted six children besides the subject of this sketch, namely, Lydia, John, Nathaniel, Sally, Betsey and Hannah.

During the Revolutionary War the schools of that town greatly deteriorated and after attending there a short time he was sent to Andover. Like all boys he was fond of play and on one occasion, while snow-balling with his mates, he was struck accidentally in the eye which was so injured that after a few years he lost the entire use of it.

Dr. Spaulding early determined to become a physician, and after leaving Andover proceeded to fit himself for college, under the tutorship of Rev. Mr. Allen of Chelmsford.

Dr. Rufus Wyman of that town, however, urged him to give up college, and enter the office of some physician, feeling that the experience thus gained would be of more value than a college training. This the young man decided to do, and went to Amherst, N. H., where he began the study of medicine with his cousin, Dr. Mathias Spaulding, who besides having great skill in his profession was also a profound scholar along other lines. It was owing to the influence of this man that Dr. Stillman Spaulding resumed his original purpose of having a college education. Dr. Mathias Spaulding had graduated with honor from Harvard in 1798 in a class having among its members such men as Stephen Longfellow, Rev. Dr. Channing and Judge Story. The atmosphere of learning into which the young man was thrown at his cousin's changed his purpose, for soon after he returned to Chelmsford, and after studying for a while with Dr. Rufus Wyman, entered Middlebury College, from which he was graduated in 1810 at the age of 22.

After leaving college he practised medicine for a few months with Dr. Morrill of Cambridge, and the next year, 1811, moved to Lexington.

During his student life at Chelmsford, he became engaged to Susan Butterfield, daughter of Capt. John and Rebecca (Kendall) Butterfield of Chelmsford. She was a girl of beautiful character and high aspirations, but she died during their courtship, and sometime later he became engaged to and finally married her sister, Lucy Butterfield.

When he first came to Lexington he boarded at the old Buckman Tavern, where he remained till his marriage.

During this time he made frequent excursions to Chelmsford to visit Miss Butterfield, and on the 13th day of May, 1819, they were married at her father's house. Soon after the wedding they came to Lexington and moved into the house known for so many years as the Spaulding Homestead on the corner of Massachusetts Avenue and Clark Street and in which he lived till his death.

Before Dr. Spaulding moved into this house a Mr. Dickson kept a grocery store in the half on the south-east side, and later Mr. Gilman. Part of the time the Spauldings occupied but one half the house, renting the other side.

The double house standing between the Spaulding Homestead and Mr. Spaulding's store is of comparatively recent date, for at the time he purchased the property, the site of the present house was an open field, sloping abruptly towards the south-west, and the present sidewalk was not then in existence. In August, 1835, Dr. Spaulding engaged the late David Tuttle to build this house, the Doctor furnishing the lumber and Mr. Tuttle performing the labor. The building was but partly finished that year, and it was not completed till sometime later. It was first rented to a man by the name of Haskell, who carried on a book-bindery for some years; later to one Sealey, a tailor from Woburn, who afterwards moved into a small building on the land of David Johnson, now the site of Miss Clara Harrington's house. This little shop was a few years later moved away by Isaac Mulliken. After Sealey left the Doctor's new house, three other tailors lived there, and still later a man named Gossum kept an oyster saloon there.

A well was dug in front of this house, now covered by the sidewalk, and probably few people know when passing there, that but a few feet of earth separate them from what is still a fine well of water.

After four years of married life Dr. Spaulding's first child was born, John Butterfield Spaulding, June 29, 1823, who lived but nine years, dying March 4, 1832. This child was a prodigy, and his father was justly proud of him.

When but eight years old, he was proficient in Latin, being able both to speak and to write it, and in other branches he was equally advanced. It was Dr. Spaulding's greatest delight to question his son in his different studies, and often, when driving out of the yard, on seeing the boy at play, he would alight from his chaise to talk with him in Latin or ask him some puzzling question in mathematics.

The death of this child was a great blow to his parents. They had four other children, (1) Susan Butterfield, born July 31, 1826, who married William Jackson Currier, M.D., January 23, 1845, and died February 24, 1877; (2) Nathaniel Edward, born November 23, 1829, who married Henrietta D. Palfrey of Boston, January 14, 1858, and died in April 1889; (3) Louisa Butterfield, born February 16, 1834, and died the next day; and (4) John Butterfield, born September 11, 1836, married Mary B. Saville of Gloucester, Mass., October 3, 1861.

Dr. Spaulding was very charitable. It mattered little to him that patients were unable to pay. They received the same tender devoted care which he gave to all others.

When the youngest child was six years old, he had Mr. Healy of Paris, a very noted portrait painter, paint the picture of each member of his family. Mr. Healy returned to America in 1860, visiting Lexington, and called on Dr. Spaulding in order to view his early work.

The Doctor was a great reader, a thorough scholar and a skillful practitioner. As a member of the Massachusetts Medical Society and a close observer of its proceedings, his mind was in touch with the most advanced medical thought of the day, and this higher knowledge which came to him found full expression throughout his professional life.

A devoted student, with a tenacious memory, his mind was stored with historic as well as scientific data. Such was his passion for reading that often, after retiring, he would re-light his candle and read for hours. On account of his poor sight, he was obliged to hold his book very near the light, and so absorbed would he become in his reading that often the flame of the candle would scorch the leaf of the book before he noticed it. His poor sight made him the object of many practical jokes at the hands of his son-in-law, the late Dr. Currier. Dr. Spaulding always burned candles, and on taking them down from the shelf one evening to light he found, after burning a number of matches, that his son-in-law had substituted two parsnips for the original tallow dips.

Dr. Spaulding was a lover of nature and took great interest and delight in agriculture. He bought at an early period about twelve acres of land lying on the top of Concord Hill, bordered on the two sides by the main Concord Road and Hill Street; also a strip of land lying on the south-east side of Belfry Hill, now owned by Mr. Chandler Richardson. On these two pieces of land he had his garden. The late Mr. Benjamin Gleason, who then lived on Concord Hill, in a house owned by Mr. David Johnson, now the site of the present Almshouse, was his gardener, and every fall after harvest Mr. Gleason took several wagon-loads of produce to Boston. Dr. Spaulding at one time kept a yoke of speckled oxen, and besides his regular practice as a physician engaged in the wood business.

So far as I have been able to learn Dr. Spaulding never held any town office, but in 1820 was one of a committee of three chosen by the town to build a fence around the Common, and in 1822 he was appointed one of the trustees of the Lexington Academy.

In politics he was a Whig, and very decided in his opinions. He was a deeply interested believer in the Swedenborgian faith, reading many books on that special subject.

He was also a member of the Hiram Lodge of Free and Accepted Masons, joining at the time it held its meetings in the Munroe Tavern.

An affection of the heart had for some time warned him of the approaching end, and he placed his affairs in order accordingly. The last entry in his day book, was at the end of the last leaf.

On the morning of his death he visited a patient in Burlington and, returning home, he dined and subsequently called at the house of his daughter. At four o'clock, an hour before his death, he put on his hat and went down the street to visit another patient. Returning to his house, he sat for a few minutes at the back porch, reading, when his attention was called to some cattle breaking into the garden. He threw down his newspaper, hurriedly walked over to the garden and fell, dead. Being missed, Mr. Johnson, his neighbor, searched for him, and in the twilight he was found peacefully lying beneath an apple tree, with his horse "Pompey" grazing nearby.

He had reached the allotted age of man, and at the close of a sweet spring day, May 28, 1860, when the sun was near its setting, his soul had quietly passed on.

Though Dr. Spaulding had his faults as many large-souled men do, his generous and kindly deeds, his hearty good cheer and inspiring words will always live in the hearts of those who knew him. To these the memory of Dr. Spaulding will be most pleasant.

His funeral took place from the Unitarian Church, Tuesday, May 31, 1860, and was attended by a large number of people. His remains rest in the new cemetery.

THE PARISH OF CAMBRIDGE FARMS.

READ BY REV. C. A. STAPLES, DECEMBER 8, 1891.

The territory now known as Lexington was, originally, a part of Cambridge. When the first settlements were made within its borders, we are unable to determine. Certainly as early as 1642, since, in the conveyance of a 600 acre tract to Herbert Pelham, in that year, embracing a large portion of what is now Lexington village, mention is made of a dwelling house thereon. Tradition says that a sawmill had been erected at that time on the brook below East Lexington, one of the earliest if not the earliest in the Massachusetts Colony. The growth of the settlement was, undoubtedly, very slow and, forty years later, the number of families located within the limits of this portion of Cambridge did not exceed thirty. The territory had been granted or sold, in large tracts, by the Cambridge proprietors, principally to Cambridge people who resided there but cultivated lands here, raising their grain, vegetables and hay on the fields which they had cleared, and drawing their wood and timber from the forests. Gradually these tracts were divided into farms and given to their children, who settled on them or sold them to men who removed here from the older towns. Thus, these lands naturally came to be designated "The Farms," "Cambridge Farms" or "Cambridge North Farms," and the people living here as "The Farmers." Even in official documents from the General Court, they are so called.

Of course the inhabitants were all taxed to support the Church at Cambridge and were required to attend meeting there on the Sabbath unless they had obtained leave to attend in some adjoining town more convenient to them. Some were connected with the Watertown and some with the Concord Church. We can hardly imagine the hardships which Church attendance often involved, the people riding on horseback a distance of seven or eight miles, or in an ox-cart, over roads that were mere paths cut through the woods, in cold and stormy weather, sometimes through deep snow or mud. Yet, every person, not disabled by sickness or old age, was required to go. Children were not allowed to grow up without religious instruction and care, and settlements beyond a certain distance from the meeting-house were discouraged and even prohibited in some towns. All must live within the sound of "the church-going bell" or of the meeting-house drum.

Attendance at Cambridge had become so grievous a burden to the farmers that, in 1682, they petitioned the General Court to be made a separate parish, having their own church and minister. It involved no change of their relation to Cambridge as a town, but permitted them to tax themselves for the maintenance of a minister and the building of a meeting-house and relieved them from paying a tax, for these purposes, to Cambridge. In all other respects they would still be under the jurisdiction of Cambridge. This petition was signed by eight of the principal men of the settlement, viz : James Cutter, Matthew Bridge, David Fiske, Sr., Samuel Stone, Sr., Francis Whitmore, John Tidd, Ephraim Winship and John Winter; but, through the position of Cambridge, unwilling to give up the tax which the farmers paid towards the support of the Cambridge minister, it was denied. Two years later, the petition was renewed and the General Court appointed a committee to consider the matter and report what action ought to be taken regarding it. Their report was favorable to the petitioners and recommended the formation of a new parish for their accomodation; but Cambridge was again able to defeat the measure. Seven years longer the farmers waited, patiently going to Cambridge to meeting, the nearest of them being five miles distant, when they again renewed their petition. Both parties were heard, and, after due consideration, the prayer for a separate parish was granted, and, on December 15, 1691, the act creating it became a law. No name was given to the parish in the act itself, but, from that time, it became known as the North Parish in Cambridge, or commonly, as the Parish of Cambridge Farms. The boundaries began, as the record says, at the water or swampy place where is a kind of bridge, south of the house of Francis Whitmore, and running south-west and north-east between Watertown and Woburn, setting off all the land north of it which belonged to Cambridge. This was, substantially, the territory now comprised in the town of Lexington. The house of Francis Whitmore must have been near the present residence of Mr. Alderman.

Such was the original North Parish in Cambridge, or Cambridge Farms, as constituted by the General Court, Dec. 15, 1691. The first meeting under this act did not take place, however, until the 22d, of April, 1692, when the people met and chose David Fiske, Sr., as the clerk of the Parish to record the votes. They resolved to invite Mr. Benjamin Estabrook to preach for them for one year from May 1, 1692, and a committee was appointed to communicate the action of the parish and receive his answer. Previous to this, the work of building a meeting-house had been commenced, and, during the year 1692, it was prepared for the occupancy of the parish. At what time the first service was held in it, we have no means of knowing.

Nothing is said of a dedication. It was used for worship when only partially finished, a plain, barnlike structure, covered with rough boards and shingle roof, without steeple or paint. Inside the church there was neither plaster nor paint. The timbers were all exposed. Rude benches extended across from the middle aisle, on either side, to the outer aisles: on one side sat the men, on the other, the women, all placed according to their supposed importance in the parish, measured by their property, age and social position. The boys were on a bench in the rear where they might be inspected. There were galleries on three sides and men's stairs and women's stairs leading to them. Subsequently, upper galleries were added, and the inside ceiled up with boards. William Reed was allowed to put in "a settee" for Goodwife Reed, and several of the men built "handsome seats, against the wall" for their wives, though not allowed to sit with them. This structure stood at the junction of Massachusetts Avenue and Bedford Street, not on the Common, but below it, where the Memorial Fountain now stands, and fronted down Massachusetts Avenue. It had three outside doors, no porches, no means of warming it, few windows and many crevices for ventilation. The original cost, as shown by the subscription paper, was between £60 and £70. Twenty-two different family names appear on the list of subscribers, forty-three in all, pledging sums from 10s, the lowest, to 2£ 12s, the highest. Thirteen of these names are represented in Lexington, now, by their descendants or persons bearing similar names.

In this meeting-house Benjamin Estabrook, a graduate of Harvard in the class of 1690, son of Rev. Joseph Estabrook of Concord, began his ministry as the preacher of Cambridge Farms, in May 1692, and continued until his death, in July 1697, when but twenty-six years of age. He was not regularly ordained and settled, however, until more than four years after he began preaching here, viz: in October, 1696, probably because the people were unable to make suitable provision for a life-settlement, every minister then being settled for life. He received £40 a year, half money and half in other pay at money prices, which shall be "for his salary and his entertainments." A house was built for him on the land now owned by Mr. William Plumer, and presented to him on the condition of his "abiding with us till God's Providence otherwise dispose of him." Mr. Estabrook died shortly after his ordination and settlement, to the great disappointment and grief of the people; evidently, a young man of fine promise and sincerely beloved by his parishioners.

After a few months he was succeeded by Rev. John Hancock, who preached for some time on probation and then received a call to settle over the parish. He accepted it and was ordained in November, 1698, as the second minister, and held the office until his death in 1752, a period of fifty-four years. John Hancock was a native of Cambridge, son of Nathaniel, the Cordwainer, and a graduate of Harvard in the class of 1689. He appears to have spent several years in teaching, before he came here, while preparing for the ministry, preaching, also, in Medford and in Groton for some time. According to agreement with the parish he was to receive £80 for a settlement, as it was termed, and £45 a year with a quarterly collection. This was, afterwards, advanced to £60 a year; but the depreciation of the currency went steadily on until the salary was hardly half that sum in good money.

In 1698, Mr. Hancock bought twenty-five acres of land of Benjamin Muzzey, lying on both sides of what is now Hancock Street, and, soon after, built the small, one story, gambrel-roof house now forming the ell of the Hancock-Clark house. He married Elizabeth, daughter of Rev. Thomas Clark, minister of Chelmsford, and, in that humble cottage their five children were born and grew up to manhood and womanhood, ultimately filling a large place in the history of the town, the state and the nation. Two of the sons graduated at Harvard. John and Ebenezer became ministers and a third son, Thomas, became the great Boston merchant, who bought Beacon Hill and built the famous Hancock mansion there, and also, the two story front of the old parsonage, here, for his father and mother. The daughters married clergymen and the descendants of John and Elizabeth Hancock have been among the most distinguished men and women of our country. I believe we may trace twenty-five ministers back to progenitors connected, in some way, with that venerable house, besides physicians, lawyers and authors.

In 1713, the parish of Cambridge Farms became the town of Lexington, and, thenceforth, the affairs of the church were managed by the town, like the schools, the roads and the poor.

The first meeting-house had become dilapidated, though it had stood only about twenty years, and, accordingly, it was voted "to under-prop the great beams, mend the leaky places, and build a new one in convenient time, after the new mode like Concord." No bell had been used to call the people together for worship up to the year 1700; probably a drum was used for that purpose. The town then voted to ask Cambridge for the bell, probably an old one, no longer in use there and the request appears to have been granted. "A turriott" was erected to hang it on — probably a belfry placed on the ground.

In due time the new meeting-house was built, costing about £500, and was first occupied in October 1714 : a much more spacious, comfortable and elegant edifice than the old one, but, apparently, of the same general appearance. It was 40 by 50 feet on the ground, and 28 feet in height, with two tiers of galleries on three sides, in the upper of which the town's powder was kept, and the negroes seated on Sunday. It had three tiers of windows and three outside doors and was unpainted outside and inside, excepting the pulpit, the front of the galleries and the pillars supporting them which, we are told, were colored. Like its predecessor, it had no steeple and no provision for warming. Here Mr. Hancock preached until his death and here his funeral was held after his long ministry had come to an end. The town generously granted £400, O.T. and observed the event by copious eating and drinking at the public houses, providing mourning weeds, gloves and rings for bearers and relatives, and digging and bricking up the grave; bills for which appear on the town records. In 1734, Ebenezer Hancock, his youngest son, had been ordained and settled as his colleague. For several years he taught the Grammar School in the town and "assisted his honored father," as the record tells us ; a young man of large promise and noble nature, whom the people regarded with great respect and esteem, and whose death, in his 30th year, after six years of service, was sincerely mourned.

Little is told in our records regarding the forms of worship in Mr. Hancock's time. The singing was by the congregation, the deacon giving out two lines at a time and the people singing them after him. The Bible was not read as a part of the service. This custom, now universal, was not introduced into the churches until long afterwards. No musical instruments were used in the service and the worship must have been destitute of beauty or variety and, hence, uninteresting and tedious to the young. Two long prayers, a long sermon, generally read from manuscript, and two of the psalms sung to dolorous tunes and without much regard for time or harmony.

Every Sunday there were two such services, with an hour's intermission. This was spent by the men at some public house, discussing the news of the day or the morning sermon, and enlivened by copious draughts of flip always in readiness for the occasion. In the meeting-house, during service, tything men were stationed at different points, provided with long poles to keep the boys in order and to break up the slumbers of ungodly men. During the intermission men were placed in the galleries to see that there was no irreverent conduct, and, at one time, a paper was given the minister to read, regulating the coming down stairs. There were no pew rents, the expenses being paid by a tax assessed on all the property of the town.

While no paper of a worldly or secular concernment was allowed posted on the meeting house, lest the house be defiled, or as it is sometimes expressed be "damnified thereby," all town meetings were held in it, except on very cold days, when adjournment was made to some tavern where the people could keep warm. Such were some of the customs prevalent in Mr. Hancock's time, which are noticed upon our records.

After the old minister's death, three years passed away in hearing candidates, before a choice was made of Jonas Clarke as his successor, a native of Newton and a graduate of Harvard in the class of 1753. He was ordained in November, 1755, and remained the minister of Lexington until his death in 1805, a period of fifty years; a bold, strong, progressive man, of untiring industry in his work and unflagging zeal in the cause of American Independence. Marrying the granddaughter of his predecessor, Lucy Bowes, daughter of the minister at Bedford, he began house-keeping in the old parsonage, and, after the death of Madam Hancock, in 1760, bought the place of Thomas, the princely Boston merchant. Here their twelve children, six sons and six daughters were born, and lived to attain the years of adult life. Here Mr. and Mrs. Clarke spent the remaining years of life, and the last of the family, two unmarried daughters, died there in 1843. Thus the Hancocks and the Clarkes occupied the place nearly 150 years. It was the rallying point of the patriot statesmen of this region during the Revolutionary period, for consultation upon the momentous affairs of the country. It was, also, a visiting place for distinguished scholars and literary men from the college and the city, and of the clergy in this portion of Middlesex County. The best society of the town and of the colony often met within its walls and around the hospitable board of "the patriot priest" as Mr. Clarke was called. Four of his daughters married ministers, and his sons became men of note, as bankers, merchants and government officials. Thus the old house became a fountain of good influences which flowed out, far and wide, making the common life more rich in culture, refinement and virtue.

Forty years of Mr. Clarke's ministry were passed in the second meeting house, erected in 1714, and standing on the Common at the time of the battle, with the belfry standing near it. In it he was ordained and in it he preached those stirring sermons which roused the spirit of resistance to injustice that proved so strong in his people when the time of trial came. But the event which has invested that meeting house with the deepest interest is that of the 19th of

April, 1775, when a little company of Lexington farmers were drawn up behind it, to defend their rights with their lives. What a scene it witnessed on that eventful morning, — seventy or eighty men, hastily summoned from their homes, standing there, in their homespun clothing, armed with their old fowling pieces, to face a battalion of the best disciplined troops in the world, and ready to lay down their lives for justice and liberty, for home and country, and the rights of mankind! And into that old meeting house were borne the bodies of the slain and laid upon the floor of its aisles, after the bloody work was done. Tradition tells us that a woman, returning from market to her home in Carlisle, on that morning after the British had marched on towards Concord, came to the Common, dismounted from her horse, went into the Church and saw the bodies lying there. What a scene the funeral must have been, in the old meeting house, when Mr. Clarke spoke of the awful tragedy in which ten of his parishioners had perished and whose bodies lay before him in the place where, on the previous Sabbath, they had joined in the worship! Above his head, as he stood in the pulpit, was the hole in the window where a cannon ball passed through the house, burying itself in the ground a few rods behind him; and before him were gathered a great multitude from this and the surrounding towns, to join in the solemn services. What wonder if words of bitterness were spoken and purposes of vengeance were kindled by that awful scene!

But nothing could save the old meeting house. These stirring memories seem to have counted for little towards preserving it from destruction. Were it standing today we would gladly cover it with gold to keep it from decay and save it for the generations to come. Governor Hancock, whose service in the cause of Independence had done so much to invest it with undying interest, whose grandfather had preached in it for forty years, and whose father was christened in it on the first Sunday after his birth, led the way for its destruction by offering to give the town $100 towards building a new one,— the record says " as soon as they struck ax to timber" in its construction. Even Parson Clarke joined in the crusade against the venerable house by adding $30 to Governor Hancock's gift. And so, after eighty years of service in the sheltering of patriotism and religion, it was pulled down, to give place to a much larger, more costly and elegant structure, the third meeting house of Lexington, built in 1794 and dedicated January 15, 1795. Evidently the people were very proud of their new house of worship and of the Bible which Governor Hancock gave, to be read in the service, and which the people accepted on the promise of Mr. Clarke, that the reading should not increase the length of the service, as one of the deacons declared that he wanted to get home and do his chores before dark. The third meeting house was regarded as a noble edifice, far more comfortable than the old one, with a lofty steeple, three spacious vestibules and a large bell which could be heard all over the town, ringing the people to meeting, ringing them to bed at nine o'clock at night, tolling when they died to tell everybody how old they were, and when their bodies were borne to the last resting place.

It had some pretentions to architectural beauty, and what doubtless pleased the people not a little was its superiority to the Concord meeting house, it being much more spacious and comfortable. Pews were placed on the floor and in the galleries, instead of long benches, and after its completion they were sold at auction, a flag being hoisted in each pew when bids were asked for, on which was inscribed " For Sail," and so well did the pews " sail " that, after paying all the cost of construction, above $2000 remained as a surplus. The house was painted a pea-green, and horse blocks were built at the doors.

In the new meeting house a choir was organized, and musical instruments, the chief of which was the great bass viol, were used to aid the singers. A singing school was established, and the town made an appropriation to buy candles and wood, to encourage the singers if they would "set" together in the gallery; and they decided to sit there. Hymn books were now procured by the people and the old custom of lineing the hymns was given up. Thus the worship in the new house during the last years of Mr. Clarke's ministry was made far more attractive and satisfactory, especially to the young people. The good old minister, active, vigorous and useful almost to the last, enjoyed the new place of worship for ten years, and in 1805 was gathered to his fathers, full of years and honors, though not of riches, as the inventory of his estate plainly shows, where the old horse is put down at $8 and the chaise at $3, each of his heirs receiving about $130. His diary closes, after fifty years of faithful keeping, with these words, " Finished haying today." The trembling hand could write no more and in a few weeks was still in death.

In December, 1807, after two years of candidating, Rev. Avery Williams was ordained as Mr. Clarke's successor, the fifth minister of Lexington. Like all his predecessors, he was settled for life; a native of Guildford, Vt., the son of Rev. Henry Williams of that town, and a graduate of Dartmouth College and Princeton Theological Seminary. He remained the minister of the town for eight years, when, on account of feeble health, incapacitating him for continuous service, he resigned and sought in the South for a renewal of his ability to labor; but it was too late.

He gradually sank under disease and died in the following year, 1816. His was the last life settlement of Lexington ministers. The town voted him $750, when the connection was dissolved, being legally bound to pay his salary as long as he lived, whether he was able to render service or not. From what we learn of Mr. Williams, he was regarded as a man of ability and worth, scholarly in his habits and tastes, and a faithful worker in this vineyard of the Lord. He lived in the old Dr. Spaulding house, at the corner of Massachusetts Avenue and Clark Street.

He was accustomed to receive boys into his family and to prepare them for college. Ezra Stiles Gannett, the famous Boston preacher, was one of the lads who passed a year in that old house under his instruction and care. Beyond the Centennial sermon, on the anniversary of the incorporation of Lexington in 1713, there is nothing remaining of his literary productions in our possession. That historical discourse is, certainly, an able and creditable piece of work, adding much to our knowledge of the early life which would otherwise have been lost. When it was preached there were those living here who remembered Parson Hancock, and nearly all the congregation had been the parishioners of Jonas Clarke. Mr. Francis Wyman was probably the last who remembered Mr. Clarke. A few still linger among us who remember Avery Williams. Four lives, therefore, easily cover the period between us and Benjamin Estabrook, the first minister of Lexington.

Rev. James Walker, afterwards pastor of the Harvard Church in Charlestown, and later, President of Harvard University, was invited to succeed Mr. Williams, but declined. Rev. Charles Briggs was finally chosen and remained the pastor until 1835, a period of sixteen years.

He was the last of the ministers whose parish included the whole town. During his ministry two other churches were organized in the town, the Baptist and the Church at East Lexington. Mr. Briggs lived in a portion of the house now belonging to Mr. James F. Russell and occupied as a hotel. He had quite a farm, extending back toward the Scotland Schoolhouse and covering the land now occupied by the village at the Crossing.

During much of the time of Mr. Briggs' ministry he was in poor health and unable to render the efficient service which the church needed. His pastorate was terminated at his own request and with the expression of kind and generous feeling on the part of the people. Rev. William G. Swett succeeded him, a man still pleasantly remembered in the town; somewhat eccentric, but of a genial spirit, fond of a good story or joke and full of sympathy and kindness. He endeared himself to the young people and was the friend and helper of all; a man of scholarly and brilliant mind. His ministry covered only three years and came to an end in 1839. His niece, a sister's daughter, is living in Florence, Italy, where she has won an honorable reputation as an artist and as an authoress. Ruskin has taken a warm interest in her career, and wrote an introduction for two or three little volumes of her sketches of Italian life and character, under the title of "Wayside Songs in Tuscany," a series of short but charming stories. The books are in the Cary Library.

After a period of five or six years, in which the pulpit was supplied by Rev. Messrs. Rice, Knapp, Crufts and Samuel J. May, the First Parish was separated wholly from the town, and incorporated as the First Congregational Society of Lexington, which is still its name. Up to that time, all its business affairs, the calling of a minister, the payment of his salary, the repairs upon the meeting-house, were transacted under town warrants, in town meeting, giving rise to endless bickering and strife. The Society was immediately reorganized, an invitation given to Rev. Jason Whitman to become its pastor and the work of improving and reconstructing the meeting-house begun. Mr. Whitman accepted the invitation and was installed in July, 1845, entering upon his ministry under the most hopeful circumstances. In the prime of life, full of enthusiasm, devoted to his work, after several years of experience in Portland and Saco, Me., with fine powers as a preacher and pastor, his ministry opened with every promise of large and high success. But after a brief service of two years and a half, he was suddenly smitten down in the midst of great usefulness and his ministry here transferred to a brighter one in the world above. The meeting-house, thoroughly repaired and refurnished, was burned to the ground on Dec. 17, 1846, just before it was to be rededicated. It was a severe blow to the Society and caused years of litigation and trouble. The Baptist Society immediately offered the use of their house, which offer was gratefully accepted and there was held the funeral of the beloved pastor, Mr. Whitman, in January, 1848.

Steps were immediately taken to erect a new house of worship, and the fourth meeting-house of the parish was built on Elm Ave., where it remains unto this day. It was dedicated Feb. 25, 1848, one month after Mr. Whitman's funeral.

Rev. Fiske Barrett succeeded Mr. Whitman in a brief ministry of nearly three years, terminated at his own request. He was followed by Rev. N A. Staples who remained for a similar period and then accepted a call to a church in Milwaukee where he ministered until the opening of the Civil War, when he entered the army as Chaplain of the Sixth Wisconsin Regiment. Here a severe illness, brought on by the exposure and hardship of camp life, broke him down so utterly that he never recovered. He became pastor of the Second Unitarian Church in Brooklyn, N. Y., where he died in February, 1864, in his thirty-third year.

Rev. Leonard J. Livermore succeeded Mr. Staples in Lexington, in October, 1857, and continued in the service of the Society for nine years, resigning in September, 1866. He afterwards became pastor of the Unitarian Church in Danvers, where he ministered until his death in June, 1886, after a pastorate of nearly twenty years.

The ministry of Rev. Henry Westcott followed that of Mr. Livermore, in Lexington, and extended from June, 1867 until June, 1881, when he resigned, a period of fourteen years. Subsequently he was installed over the Unitarian Church in Melrose, and died suddenly, after a prosperous pastorate, in June, 1883, in the prime of his years.

This brings the record down to the settlement of the present pastor, Rev. C. A. Staples, October 31, 1881, and the story, altogether, covers two full centuries.

The average length of the pastorates has been fourteen years. 2402 funerals are recorded in our church books and 664 marriages. Rev. John Hancock and his son recorded 645 funerals and 60 marriages. Rev. Jonas Clarke recorded 556 funerals of which 202, or over 36 per cent. are of infants and children, and 218 marriages.

I have recorded 238 funerals, of which barely 7 per cent. are of children under 12 years, and 59 weddings.

I quote these statistics from our records to show that a vast gain has been made in the care and preservation of child-life in these 200 years.

I wish I could show, clearly, as large a gain in the moral life of the town, and yet I am inclined to believe that it has really taken place, and I hope, sometime, to be able to prove it.

May the old parish and all other parishes in the town be ever reaching out and pressing on towards better life for body, mind and soul in their people, and a better life for the state and the nation.

CHARLES FOLLEN.
READ BY JAMES P. MUNROE, MARCH 12, 1891.

It is sometimes noted with regret, almost with apology, that Lexington has not on the rolls of her citizens such great names as those of which Concord can boast. To few towns, indeed, has it been given to shelter an Emerson and a Hawthorne; but Lexington can point to two men, besides her heroes of the Revolution, who gave themselves, heart and soul, to the progress of liberty, to the cause of the injured slave. Theodore Parker and Charles Follen died too soon to see the results of their great labors in the cause of freedom; but their names will live forever in the catalogue of those who maintained, in the face of every obstacle, the right, and who "*would* be heard."

Charles Follen, whose whole name was Karl Theodor Christian Follenius, was born in Romrod, Hesse, not far from Frankfort, September 4, 1796. His father was a counsellor-at-law at Giessen, near which Romrod is situated, and was a man of ability and influence. His mother died when he was three years old, leaving three sons — of whom Charles was the second — and a daughter. Four years later his father married again, and this stepmother showed wise and loving devotion to her husband's children. Nevertheless, Charles Follen's childhood was not happy. Of a sensitive, serious, almost morbid nature, like children of that stamp, he was little understood. He overcame this disadvantage, however, and, after passing through the usual courses of study, entered, at sixteen years of age, the University of Giessen. Just at that time, the German states having roused themselves from the paralysis of Napoleon's successes, and having been given courage, by his disastrous Russian campaign, to declare war against him, the students of the universities were called to arms. Soon after the Battle of Leipsic, Charles and his two brothers joined a rifle corps of students. Charles was not called upon to fight, but his elder brother won military distinction.

The feeling of nationality aroused by this appeal to arms against Bonaparte was not to be readily quenched. The success of the uprising against the invader had shown how much of good a union of petty principalities might accomplish; a short experience of the Code Napoléon had given some of the states a taste of representative government, and the close of the campaign against the French found the German youth ripe for revolution. The sectional spirit theretofore strong in Germany, had been greatly fostered by the organization of the university students into societies upon sectional lines. The student in Germany has a far larger influence upon politics than in America, and the rivalry and duels between members of the different corps did much to perpetuate the disunion of the Teutonic states.

In order that they might secure a larger measure of freedom for themselves and the other Germans, the wiser students saw that they must break down these silly corps barriers; and Follen early associated himself with them in forming the Burschenschaft, a union of students from all parts of Germany to oppose and destroy the sectional and partisan societies. The leaders of the old corps were highly incensed at this independent action; and they were especially bitter against Follen, who, in addition to his activity in the new society, had, by the purity and diligence of his own life, made silent protest against the prevailing license and idleness of the universities. They challenged him again and again to broadsword duels, hoping to break his spirit, but he courageously accepted all challenges, having made himself a master of athletic exercises under the training of the famous gymnast, Jung. At last the Burschenschaft was reported to the government as treasonable in its tendency, and the rectors of the universities were called upon to investigate it. Needless to say, they found no evidence of guilt. Thereupon Follen published a pamphlet setting forth the objects and acts of the Burschenschaft, a pamphlet which is interesting in that it shows him, at twenty-one, imbued with the strong love of liberty and fair play which distinguished him through life. In this same year, 1817, he received the degree of Doctor of Civil and Ecclesiastical Law.

Hardly had he begun the practice of his profession than he again took up the cause of freedom and justice. The Grand Duke of Hesse had issued a decree relative to the collection of debts, into the details of which it is unnecessary to go, but the result of which would have been to take away the last semblance of local self-government. The burgomasters of the several towns begged Follen to present a petition from them, praying that this decree be rescinded, and to argue the justice of this petition. This task Follen readily and successfully undertook, though, in doing so, he knew he forfeited all chance for promotion in his native country. Indeed, his bold course in the matter subjected him at once to persecution from the government, so that he found it advisable to leave Giessen. He went thence to Jena to lecture upon jurisprudence. He was well received in Jena; but six months after his arrival occurred the murder of Kotzebue. This poet and playwright, who was much in vogue, had, by his satire of the young German liberal party, given rise to the suspicion of being a Russian spy, in the pay of the autocratic party. Therefore a fanatic named Sand murdered him. All the friends of Sand, including Follen, were at once arrested. Follen was found, of course, innocent of all connection with the crime; yet, four months later, and in the middle of the night, he was again arrested. Examined, cross-questioned, and confronted with Sand, in the hope of proving him guilty, he was nevertheless acquitted, but was forbidden again to lecture in Jena. Finding that the influence of his father and of other powerful friends at Giessen, whither he had returned, could not save him, Follen left Germany for Paris, where he became intimate with Lafayette. There again occurred a political murder to drive him away. The Bourbon Duke de Berri was assassinated, and immediately all foreigners without definite business in France were ordered to leave the country. Follen went to Switzerland, accepted a professorship in one of the cantonal schools, but, spreading doctrines unwelcome to the Calvinist clergy, was soon asked to resign. He was then called to the University of Bâsle to lecture upon law. There he was most happily placed; but this mild youth after having suffered persecution from his fellow-students, from the Grand Duke of Hesse, from the French government and the Calvinistic synod, was now to encounter the thunders of the "Holy Alliance." Russia, Austria and Prussia, having joined, and, with England's help, put down Napoleon, now maintained their "holy" alliance for the suppression of freedom throughout Europe. On the 27th of August, 1824, the three governments sent notes to the Canton of Bâsle demanding that Follen, who ceaselessly preached liberty, be given up for trial. These notes were accompanied by a request from the government of Berne, urging Bâsle, for the sake of Switzerland's safety, to surrender him. Bâsle, however, refused. Thereupon came a second formal demand from the allied powers threatening the Republic and supplemented by notes of urgency from Berne, Zurich and Lucerne. This was too much even for courageous little Bâsle, and Follen was warned by the authorities to flee. This he refused to do, and demanded a trial; whereupon the Canton ordered his arrest. Upon this, urged by his friends, he made his escape, leaving behind him the following declaration :

"Whereas the Republic of Switzerland, which has protected so many fugitive princes, noblemen and priests, would not protect him, who, like them, is a republican, he is compelled to take refuge in the great asylum of liberty, the United States of America. His false accusers he summons before the tribunal of God and public opinion. Laws he has never violated. But the heinous crime of having loved his country has rendered him guilty to such a degree, that he feels quite unworthy to be pardoned by the Holy Alliance."

His friends assisted in every way in his escape, one taking him out of the city concealed under the boot of his chaise, another, who resembled him, giving up to him his passport, and at Havre, Captain Allen of the "Cadmus," the vessel which had just returned from taking Lafayette to America, affording him every protection.

Follen landed in New York in December, 1824, and he says : "I wanted to kneel upon the ground, and kiss it and cling to it with my hands, lest it should even then escape my grasp." How soon was he to find what a mockery our boasted freedom at that time was! Immediately upon arriving he wrote to Lafayette, who gave him letters and advised him to go to Boston. Before doing this, he devoted himself to the study of English, and was so extraordinarily successful that in less than a year he was able fluently to deliver, in Boston, a course of lectures on the Civil Law. As one reads his writings it is a matter of astonishment to note the ease and skill with which he handles our idiomatic tongue. Only once in many pages does he betray his foreign birth.

In the fall of 1825 Follen was appointed a teacher of German at Harvard College, and later he was made head of a gymnasium in Boston. He began at the same time the preparation of a grammar and reader of the German language which was subsequently in extensive use. Everywhere he met with much kindness, his intimacy with Lafayette opening to him many doors which his own worth and talents kept afterwards ajar. Soon after his arrival he met, through the introduction of his friend Miss Sedgwick, Miss Eliza Lee Cabot, to whom he was later married.

During the following winter he met Dr. Channing, who at once exerted a tremendous influence upon Follen, so much so that soon, under Channing's urgency, he decided to prepare for the ministry. To that end, he spent the Summer of 1827 at Newport studying under Channing's direction. In the following year, having meanwhile kept up his work at Harvard and in the gymnasium, he was formally admitted as a candidate for the ministry. He now not only was anxious to preach, but, having been betrothed to Miss Cabot, he was in haste to marry. By taking, in addition to his other duties, the position of instructor in Ecclesiastical History and Ethics, both wishes were realized. On September 15, 1828 he was married, and in March, 1830, to his great joy, he was naturalized a citizen of the United States.

In the Summer of 1830 he preached at Newburyport and

was invited to settle there; but just then Harvard College, upon the presentation of the sum of five hundred dollars a year for five years, had agreed to found a professorship of German Literature and to ask Follen to fill it. At last everything seemed prosperous; he had apparently an assured and honorable position, the atmosphere of Cambridge was congenial, his wife and child were well and happy. Therefore, he prepared to make this his life-work, purchased land, and built a house. But a chance conversation with a poor negro affected him so strongly that he went to see Garrison in that famous little attic printing-house, and the whole course of his life was changed. He began to realize that the Declaration of Independence was a living lie, that America was free only in name; and, less than two years later, he joined the Anti-Slavery Society, then but a year old. That he knew how much this step involved is shown by his saying to Mrs. Follen: "If I join the Anti-Slavery Society I shall certainly lose all chance of a permanent place in the College or perhaps anywhere else." Later he said: "I did not feel at liberty to stand aloof from a Society whose only object was the abolition of slavery." Shortly afterwards, in January, 1834, he was chosen chairman of a committee to draft an address on the subject of slavery. It is a splendid piece of writing, clear, calm, logical, pitiless in its serenity. It never stoops to invective, never appeals to passion, but finds its arguments in the Declaration of Independence, in the natural rights of man, in human justice. In summing up, he says, in part: "You who believe in the Gospel of redemption, you who believe that the day will come when we must all appear before the judgment-seat of Christ, how will you stand before Him who tries and judges the heart? . . . When a band of those, who in your day and generation were kept in slavery, shall rise on the right hand of the Judge to witness against you, do you think that the testimony of the colored man, rejected here, will be rejected also in the Court of Eternal Justice? Or do you believe that you may evade the sentence of the Judge by pleading that you attended to all the bodily wants and comforts of the slave, . . . when you refused food and clothing, freedom, respect and love to the immortal soul? Or, do you think yourselves safe under the plea that you yourselves were not slaveholders, . . . when in any degree it depended on your exertions to put an end to the very existence of slavery in this world?"

"You to whom the destinies of this country are committed . . . if you are Republicans, not by birth only, but from principle, then let the avenues, all the avenues of light and liberty, of truth and love, be opened wide to every soul within the nation, — that the bitterest curse of millions may no longer be that they were born and bred in 'the land of the free and the home of the brave.'"

During these years he was warned again and again that the public expression of his opinions would ruin his prospects at Harvard. His only answer was: "Is this my duty? What will be its consequences is a secondary matter." The warnings were too true. At the end of the five years when the original subscription to found the professorship of German literature had expired, he asked if his position was to be continued. The answer came that it was considered inexpedient, but that he might, if he chose, resume his original place as a teacher of German, at $500 a year. He could not, of course, accept this humiliating proposal, and, after ten years of faithful service to the college, he must again look for means to earn his bread. He planned to start a school, but poverty forbade. He lectured, gave lessons and preached here and there, among other places in East Lexington. The first recorded meeting of the people there for public worship was on April 5, 1835, and, on that and the following two Sundays, Charles Follen preached. Ralph Waldo Emerson probably had preached earlier, as he did later, to the people of the village, though the record, beyond that of tradition, is not preserved.

Just as his professorship expired, Mr. Follen received an invitation to superintend the education of the sons of Mr. James Perkins. He accepted the offer, as it promised competence and freedom, but, in doing so, he wrote at some length to their guardian, setting forth his views on education and the manner in which he purposed dealing with these boys. In this letter he says:

. . . "If I undertook the superintendence of their education. . . . I should feel bound to educate them not only for college but for life; I should study their natures, awake every dormant energy, cherish every generous sentiment, and lead them to form such habits and tastes as would qualify them to act an honorable part in those relations in life which they would be called upon to sustain. I should endeavor not only to furnish them with general information, but to discover any individual talent and taste that, by proper cultivation, might give to their pursuits in after life a decided direction to some practical object. For I believe that to a young man called to the possession of wealth there is no temptation so great as that which arises from having no decided object in life, no pursuit that occupies his mind in his many hours of leisure."

This arrangement was a very happy one, and the life of the Follens and their three young charges at Watertown and at Milton, was wholly satisfactory; but at the end of a year the necessity of dividing his authority with others impelled Dr. Follen to relinquish this congenial task. His almost morbid conscience would not allow him to continue in an arrangement that did not permit of his doing his duty, as he saw it, to the fullest extent.

During this happy year the Follens became intimate with Harriet Martineau, who was making her well-known journey through the United States. Her influence, together with that of the mobbing of Garrison, moved Dr. Follen to even bolder expression of his anti-slavery views. On January 20, 1836, he made a stirring address before the Anti-Slavery Society in support of the following resolutions: "Resolved, That we consider the anti-slavery cause as the cause of philanthropy, with regard to which all human beings, white men and colored men, citizens and foreigners, men and women, have the same duties and the same rights." This he advocated in opposition to the movement to exclude negroes, foreigners and women from fellowship in the work.

Soon thereafter the Governor of Massachusetts, in his annual message, censured the abolitionists; the legislatures of some of the Southern States formally asked that they be suppressed, and action was therefore taken. A committee of the General Court was appointed to investigate their doings and to recommend procedure. The Anti-Slavery Society immediately appointed a committee to appear before this legislative committee, and, if possible, to avert action against the abolitionists. For this duty were chosen Garrison, May, Ellis Gray Loring, William Goodell and Charles Follen.

The following summer was spent at Stockbridge. While there, an invitation came from the parish of the First Unitarian Church of New York City to preach to them. This offer he accepted, and October 30, 1836, he was ordained at Dr. Channing's church in Boston, Mr. Caleb Stetson preaching the ordination sermon. Follen was greatly beloved in his New York parish and all went well until Thanksgiving Day, when, in the course of his sermon, he touched upon slavery. His remarks disturbed and angered many of the congregation, two members leaving with much ostentation. Only a few lines setting forth truths perfectly obvious then as now; but courageous words to utter before a New York audience in 1836! Their result was shown at the meeting of the pewholders six months later. Of this Dr. Follen's diary says: "Meeting of pewholders: result of vote, Shall Dr. F. be invited to remain with us?— Yeas, 27; nays, 16." Nevertheless it was so strongly represented to him that the better parishioners wished him to remain that he consented to stay a year longer. A busy, useful year it was. Not only was his preaching satisfactory, but the influence of himself and his wife upon the parish and in behalf of the poor was productive of the highest good. He continued, however, to speak fearlessly against slavery, and at the expiration of this second year the opposition to his ministry had gained such strength that he declined to be a candidate for the permanent pastorate of the church.

He returned to Boston and occupied himself in lecturing, in occasional preaching and in writing a book which he had long had in view,— a treatise on psychology. He formed plans, too, for a journey to Switzerland in the summer, being assured that it was safe for him to return there. His arrangements for this holiday were already made when he received an urgent request from the society at East Lexington to become their minister for a year if possible, or at least for six months. They represented to him that they were too poor to pay more than a very small salary, but that, unless he came to gather them together, the feeble parish would fall to pieces. With his usual spirit of self-sacrifice and in a hope that he might, perhaps, found here an ideal, unsectarian, Christian church, he gave up his cherished trip to Switzerland and accepted the call to East Lexington.

He had stipulated that he should not be held to the usual parish duties, and he hoped now to carry out his long-deferred plan of finishing his treatise on psychology. A large and comfortable house — that just beyond the present church — had been taken for him, the people of the parish lent ready hands to put it in order, and once more his beloved books, so many times packed away in his various changes of residence, were spread around him. He looked forward to a long summer of literary work; but at once his active, sympathetic nature became deeply concerned in the affairs of the village, the earnest project for erecting a meeting-house enlisted his heartiest interest, and almost immediately he found himself wholly engaged in preparing plans for the building, in begging assistance from his many wealthy and influential friends, and in helping the people make preparations for the great fair that was to add materially to the building fund. So active was his parish that on the Fourth of July after his arrival, ground was broken for the new edifice. He was immensely interested in its progress, watching its growth from day to day with a pleasure doubled by the fact of his being its architect. He had highest hopes and plans for his adopted town and had induced some of his friends, should he remain, to build in East Lexington, as he himself had made his preparations to do. It is said that among these friends was Wendell Phillips, who had selected a site. So great was the power of Follen's strong, gentle nature over every one with whom he came in contact, that, had he been spared to live and work in East Lexington, his influence upon our town would undoubtedly have been most extraordinary. That his presence here for less than a year made so deep and lasting an impression is sufficient proof of this.

Finally the church building was so far advanced that preparations were made for its dedication. Follen writes to Dr. Channing, under date of October 11, 1839: "My affairs in this village are essentially the same. The people have formed themselves into a society under the name of the Christian Association of East Lexington. They have passed a vote to request me to continue with them, promising to increase my salary as soon as it is in their power. The new church will be ready for dedication probably about the middle or the latter part of November. It is to be a temple of freedom, and as such, commends itself to you, and I trust it will be dedicated by you to its service."

But the building was somewhat delayed, and, having been asked to give a course of lectures in New York, which would necessitate an absence of several weeks, the dedication was postponed until January 15, 1840. Mrs. Follen and their son accompanied him to New York. Soon after their arrival Mrs. Follen was taken dangerously ill and it was soon evident that it would be impossible for her to return to Lexington in time for the dedication. He wrote at once, therefore, to the committee of the church, asking that the ceremony be postponed a week, representing to them not only that Mrs. Follen's absence would be a matter of regret to him, but also that it would be necessary for him to return to New York for her should they find it impossible to defer the dedication. He left the question, however, entirely to their decision, and, most unhappily as events proved, the committee concluded that it was not for the best interests of the church to delay its opening. Dr. Follen, though much disappointed, appreciated their position and cheerfully made his preparations for the journey. The steamboat "Lexington" on which he had gone to New York, was considered very unsafe ; therefore, to satisfy Mrs. Follen, who had unhappy forebodings of disaster, he made every inquiry concerning the vessel, only to meet assurances from those competent to judge, of her entire safety. He set off, however, with a heavy heart, deciding at the last moment not to take his son who, it had been planned, should accompany him. The "Lexington" left New York on Monday. Dr. Follen not having arrived on Wednesday, and all preparations having been made, the dedication services were regretfully held without him. The next day came the dreadful news that the "Lexington" had been burned in Long Island Sound, and that only four of all those on board had been rescued. Dr. Follen was not among the saved. On the 13th of January, 1840, before he had reached his forty-fourth year, this great soul which had done so much and in whose power it was to do so much more for humanity, was, through dreadful bodily torture, taken away.

Follen was not, apparently, a great preacher. His mind was of that German type which is slow, painstaking, insistent upon details, and profoundly metaphysical. His earlier discourses were too transcendental for the ordinary mind ; and, when he appreciated his mistake, he went, perhaps, too far in the opposite direction, dwelling exhaustively upon minor things. He is criticised, on the one hand, for being difficult to understand, and, on the other, of leading the mind too slowly from point to point of his argument. He labored, moreover, under the disadvantage of foreign birth, in that he was slow of speech and precise to a fault in his delivery. But these are petty matters. It was the man himself who conquered. It was his personality that brought every one connected with him so completely under his gentle sway. His face betrays the secret of his power, that face which Whittier describes:

> "The calm brow through the parted hair,
> The gentle lips which knew no guile,
> Softening the blue eyes' thoughtful care
> With the bland beauty of their smile."

Humanly speaking, he was almost absolutely good. His nature was so thoroughly rounded that it seems contradictory; one may speak of it as an antithesis. He was absolutely fearless, yet gentle as a little child; stern and uncompromising toward the wrong, yet mild and forbearing as a saint. He was positive and unshakable in his beliefs, yet courteous and tolerant to all; exquisitely refined, almost womanish in his tastes, yet closely sympathetic with the beggared and outcast. He was extraordinarily domestic, so that his home life was idyllic, yet all mankind was his first and dearest charge. He was metaphysical, almost mystical, and nevertheless, in matters of daily life, of homely help and training, he was intensely practical. In short, he was the ideal man, combining moral, intellectual and physical attributes rarely found united in one person. If his short life was unsuccessful it was from no lack of the qualities which make for honest and enduring success. He failed, if one calls it failure, because he was ahead of his time, and because he would not bend principle to expediency. He was cheerful and contented under adversity and misrepresentation, not because he was mean-spirited, but because his lofty nature could not lose its sunniness. He had a sort of serene and holy persistency that, he knew, would conquer in the end; he believed in the final triumph of right and he was content to wait. That he would have triumphed had he lived it is impossible to doubt.

What Lexington lost by his untimely death it is idle to speculate upon. How great a blow the anti-slavery cause received it is easier to see. The cause needed just such men as he, — cool, logical, careful of the prejudices of others but, none the less, fearless and burning with zeal. He was opposed, as Channing and many others were opposed, to Garrison's methods, and he would have supplied, perhaps, more than any one else could supply, the qualities of temper which were wanted to balance Garrison's vehemence. He could not have failed to be a conspicuous and commanding figure in the momentous years which followed his death. But, like Koerner, the poet whom in his youth he knew and loved, he died before his work could be accomplished. Follen's last writing was to translate, in East Lexington, a poem written by Koerner as he lay dying on the battlefield. It is singularly fitted to Dr. Follen himself, and with this beautiful thought we will leave him :

> "This smarting wound,— these lips so pale and chill,—
> My heart, with faint and fainter beating, says,
> I stand upon the border of my days.
> Amen. My God, I own Thy holy will.
> The golden dreams that once my soul did fill,
> The songs of mirth become sepulchral lays.
> Faith! Faith! That truth which all my spirit sways,
> Yonder, as here, must live within me still ;
> And what I held as sacred here below,
> What I embraced with quick and youthful glow,
> Whether I called it liberty or love,
> A seraph bright I see it stand above ;
> And, as my senses slowly pass away,
> A breath transports me to the Realms of Day."

ORIGIN OF THE LEXINGTON AND WEST CAMBRIDGE BRANCH RAILROAD.

READ BY GEORGE Y. WELLINGTON, DECEMBER, 13, 1898.

The early history of the Lexington and West Cambridge Railroad, before the organization under its charter, has been prepared from the original papers, in the possession of the late William Wilkins Warren, who took an active part in the proceedings of the citizens of West Cambridge [now Arlington]. To them belongs the credit of originating the measures which led to the realization of the enterprise.

The success of branch roads and their benefit to towns, instancing the Woburn Branch, caused the subject to be agitated among a few of the leading and influential citizens of West Cambridge, early in 1844. Especially from the fact that it required less than two miles of road to be built from a point on the Charlestown Branch Railroad in Cambridge, with terminus opposite the Hotel on Main Street, West Cambridge, without crossing it or creating any considerable amount of land damage. The stock would all readily be taken up in the town.

The first public meeting held was in response to a printed hand-bill signed "A Citizen," and dated September 16, 1844, of which the following is a copy: WEST CAMBRIDGE BRANCH RAILROAD. "The citizens of West Cambridge one and all are invited to meet at the Parish Hall in said town on Monday evening next, September 23, at 7 o'clock, to consider the expediency of adopting measures for a branch railroad either from the Fresh Pond or Fitchburg Railroads to the centre of the town. A general attendance is expected, as it is deemed by many a subject of vast importance to the town."

Pursuant to this notice a large number attended the meeting, at which Col. Thomas Russell presided, and William W. Warren was chosen secretary. The Hon. James Russell, Dr. Timothy Wellington, John Schouler and several others advocated the building of the road, to terminate near the Unitarian Meeting House, with a view ultimately to having it extended to the upper part of the town, from thence to Lexington. A resolution of its expediency was adopted, and a committee of seven was appointed to get information, examine the routes, and report at a future meeting. The secretary of this committee, Mr. Warren, by an attractively printed poster, called a meeting to hear the report and adopt measures necessary to the immediate construction of the road.

At the meeting October 14, 1844, Hon. James Russell, who was chosen chairman, read a full report of the committee, which reported two routes, one east of the Pond, and one crossing the island in Spy Pond, and recommending a survey and estimate of cost, also a committee to obtain subscriptions to defray the expenses. The report was accepted and Hon. James Russell, Dr. Timothy Wellington and John Schouler were chosen as a committee on survey and drawings of the road; George C. Russell and Henry Whittemore, as a committee on estimates. The reports of these committees were made at a meeting held January 13, 1845.

The committee on survey had employed Messrs. Felton and Parker, engineers, to survey, make profiles, and give estimates, for which service seventy dollars were paid them. They had met and consulted with the president and directors of the Charlestown and Fresh Pond Railroad, who took the matter under favorable advisement, as to the proposed connection with their road, and were to have given their reply. The committee had long waited for a reply, when it was ascertained that some prominent citizens of Lexington had urged the officers of the Charlestown Branch Railroad not to commit themselves to the citizens of West Cambridge, until it should be determined whether the citizens of Lexington should or should not petition the Legislature for a railroad, over the route surveyed, to West Cambridge, to extend to Lexington. Such a project had already been determined upon, and under the circumstances, the committee asked to be discharged from the subject matter, which was done.

A petition for the West Cambridge Branch Railroad, signed by Timothy Wellington and others, and orders of notice, were passed by the Senate and the House, January 16, 1845. At a hearing on both petitions, one for the West Cambridge Branch Railroad, the other for the Lexington and West Cambridge Branch Railroad, in March, 1845, before the committee of the Legislature, Hon. George Washington Warren appeared for the Lexington petitioners and William Wilkins Warren for the West Cambridge petitioners. It was agreed by a compromise that the two enterprises be merged in one, and an act of incorporation was prepared and presented this same month, which, in the House Document No. 48, was passed under the title of the Lexington and West Cambridge Branch Railroad Company.

Under this act the first meeting of the new corporation took place at Cutler's Tavern, in Lexington, April 14, 1845. Larkin Turner was chosen president, and William Wilkins Warren secretary of the meeting. The Act of Incorporation was accepted, and a committee of nine gentlemen were chosen, consisting of Benjamin Muzzey and Samuel Chandler of Lexington, Timothy Wellington and John Schouler of West Cambridge, John Wesson and John W. Mulliken of Charlestown, Edmund Munroe and Otis Dana of Boston, and J. W. Simonds of Bedford, to cause subscription books to be opened May 1, 1845, for subscriptions to capital stock not to exceed $200,000. The meeting then adjourned to meet April 21, 1845, in the Parish Hall, West Cambridge, to confer with the citizens of this town. This conference meeting was largely attended and indicated a mutual interest and good feeling on the part of both towns. Benjamin Muzzey, who presided, and William Wilkins Warren acting as secretary, stated that no business was contemplated at this meeting, only an interchange of views desired. Estimates were discussed, and harmony prevailed in the discussion among the citizens of both towns, indicating a prompt action and successful commencement of the railroad which, by the Compromise Act, was to be finished and running from West Cambridge within one year from date of the Act, or its charter would be void. The adjournment of this meeting was the finality of the series preceding the organization of this railroad, under its charter.

This full account of the origin of the Lexington and West Cambridge Railroad, has been taken from the original reports of William Wilkins Warren, who was secretary of the different meetings; he preserved all of the original papers, and gave them, to be preserved at his death, to Mrs. Sophronia Russell; her son, Frank F. Russell, loaned them to me, and they will become the property of the Arlington Historical Society.

SOME MEMORIES
OF THE LEXINGTON CENTENNIAL.

READ BY MISS MARY E. HUDSON, FEBRUARY 13, 1900.

The year 1900, on which we have just entered, marks off a quarter of a century since Lexington celebrated her great Centennial Day. To those not personally interested, the celebration, with its great successes and its many mistakes, is fast becoming an event of ancient history. Before the memory of that day quite vanishes in the mists of antiquity, it may not be time misspent to recall briefly a few incidents connected with its observance.

There were, as you know, no women on that Centennial Committee, but one greatly overworked sub-committee, the Committee on Invitations, so far honored with an associate membership the writer of this paper as to accept, with much avidity, such degree of clerical assistance as it was in her power to render. Thus it befell that one favored woman became involved in a maze of records and of correspondence, both personal and official, from which extrication was impossible till the eventful day was over; and thus it is that, from a woman's pen, are given you these few rambling reminiscences — for they are nothing more — of Lexington's great Centennial.

Those officially authorized to do the work have given us in detail the story of the day. Out of the many memories of the busy weeks which preceded the 19th of April, 1875, I shall simply recall a few of the more prominent, as giving some poor idea of the work, worry and perplexity out of which the celebration was evolved.

Twenty-five years ago, the 19th of April had not become a public holiday. The happy day of the balloon man and the lunch wagon, the Moxie cart and the peanut stand, had not yet dawned upon our favored town. Lexington still celebrated, in her own quiet, delightful way, and with the assistance of her own personal friends, the events which had given her world-wide renown.

But the year 1875 brought the hundredth anniversary of her historic day and demanded a wider and more public recognition. A fruitless attempt was early made to arrange for a union of Lexington and Concord in a joint celebration which should be equally honorable to both. When this proved impossible, Lexington bent all her energies toward making her own observance of the day worthy of the great event to be commemorated. Out of the great committee appointed early in 1874, how many sub-divisions were made I dare not try to tell. Suffice it to say they represented every section of our town and included our most honored names in their list of members.

What problems confronted these unhappy men, what demands were made upon their time, their wisdom and their patience, only the survivors of that honorable body can now adequately understand.

It was near midwinter before matters seemed to assume any very definite shape, and I think the first really tangible achievement of the Committee was the securing of the Ancient and Honorable Artillery Company, as escort for the procession. That success meant much for Lexington. It meant that those mighty warriors, in all their martial splendor, with Brown's famous Brigade Band, should head our great procession. It also meant three hundred and fifty dinner tickets, an aggregate somewhat appalling to our thrifty dinner committee. Still Lexington's hospitality knew no stint on that memorable day, and the Ancients were made welcome to the best our town could give. I need not recall the long and anxious consultations out of which grew our great centennial procession; but one feature of that parade came very near the hearts of our people and deserves a passing mention. The Lexington Minute Men! Who does not recall, with something of the old-time enthusiasm, that beautiful vision of buff and blue, so vividly suggesting what Washington's Continentals might have been had they not been ragged and rusty and foot-sore? The career of our Minute Men was brilliant but too brief. As quickly as they rose, so speedily they disappeared. Sometimes, in these later days, when some festal anniversary makes such a costume appropriate, there still flashes before our admiring eyes, on the person of some youthful patriot, the old familiar uniform, inherited from the Centennial Day; but the Lexington Minute Men of 1875 are gone from our sight to return no more. In Cary Library is still preserved the handsome silk flag presented to the Minute Men by the descendants of Ensign Robert Munroe.

The busy winter slowly wore away, and, when April came, definite arrangements for orator, guests, transportation, dinner, procession and a score of other matters were well under way. Lexington was awakening to a realization of the undertaking in which she was engaged, and an air of mild interest and expectation became apparent among even our soberest citizens.

In this connection it is fitting and pleasant to recall the invaluable services of one member of the Committee, the late Rev. Edward G. Porter, whose busy life-work has so recently and so suddenly ended, but whose name will long be associated with so much that is best and highest in our town. With characteristic zeal and energy he worked for the Centennial, and to his wide experience, his cultured taste and his unflagging industry were due many of the most attractive and finished details of our anniversary exercises. It was his request that brought, from South Carolina, the graceful palmetto tree, to stand upon our platform, beside the Massachusetts pine; and to him, I think, was due the happy suggestion of the planting of the Centennial Elm by the hands of our honored Chief Magistrate. Mr. Porter early undertook a collection of old-time relics for exhibition on Centennial Day, and the success he met must have far outrun his most sanguine expectations. The name of those relics was legion. Their variety was endless. The untiring enthusiasm with which their collector sought, far and near, for souvenirs of the olden time warmed many a heart and opened for him many a stranger's door. Willing hands brushed the cobwebs from old, forgotten relics of bygone days, old chests gave up their long-neglected stores and long-closed attic doors swung open at his approach. Such antiquarian treasures as he gathered, for that occasion, old Lexington never saw before and may never behold again.

I pleasantly recall the eager step with which, coming straight from his own church door on that last busy Sunday noon, he walked in on the chairman of the Committee of One Hundred, and, proudly laying down a shapeless paper parcel, triumphantly exclaimed: "I've got Sam Adams' baptismal blanket!" Few knew whence all these historic treasures came. What was their after fate still fewer could definitely tell. Tags broke away from the articles they marked, and were scattered, in dire confusion, when the Centennial Day was over. Hurried hands replaced them without much regard for historic accuracy, and Surgeon Fiske's snow-shoes, marked "Spectacles of Col. William Munroe," may be cited as one among the many grotesque blunders of that hurried rearrangement. But, out of all this chaos, order came at last. Many articles were at once reclaimed by their careful owners, but some souvenirs of the greatest historic interest were generously donated to the town and became the nucleus of the valuable collection now found in Cary Library and in the cases of the Historical Society. Perhaps the most interesting of all these historic treasures were the beautiful Pitcairn pistols. They were carried by Major Pitcairn, on the march to Lexington and one of them was discharged, on Lexington Common, when he gave his famous order to fire. Later in the day, when his riderless horse galloped into the rebel lines, the pistols were still in the holsters and fell into American hands. Coming, later, into the possession of General Israel Putnam, he carried them through the Revolution, and left them as a precious legacy, to his descendants. They were exhibited in Lexington by the childless widow of the last owner, John P. Putnam of Cambridge, N. Y., and were immediately reclaimed when the day was over, but not until they had attracted the attention of General Belknap, then Secretary of War, who at once opened negotiations for their purchase for the Museum of the War Department at Washington. But the story of our Centennial had fired the patriotic heart of the venerable lady, who promptly rejected the Secretary's offer and donated the pistols to Lexington, proudly declaring, in a private communication to a member of the Committee that there were some things which money could not buy. In early autumn the pistols came back to Lexington, and are preserved in Cary Library.

The caring for the great company expected on the

19th, the planning of the great pavilion and dinner tent, were problems sorely taxing the committees having these matters in charge; but when did Lexington ever fail in hospitality? Surely not in 1875, when she raised, on the Common, a beautiful pavilion capable of accommodating seven thousand people, and a dinner tent with places for thirty-seven hundred guests. Perhaps few of our people realize that this dinner tent ran the entire length of the Elm Avenue front of the Common, crossed Bedford Street and occupied a portion of the triangular green in front of what is now Historic Hall. Some of us bewailed the necessity of cutting down a vigorous young tree, to make room for this monster tent, but, after the lapse of twenty-five years, few miss it or could recall the spot whereon it stood. These tents were works of art, in their way, very elaborately decorated with flags, streamers and flowers, but truth compels me to own they were cold and uncomfortable places. We had all heard the old story of the waving grass and blossoming peach trees which had greeted the English invaders, a hundred years before, and the warm, sunny days of early April had encouraged us to hope for similar verdure on the great anniversary day. This hope was soon and ruthlessly dispelled. At noon of Tuesday, April 13, just as the frame work of the dinner tent was being raised and the floor being laid in the pavilion, there burst upon us one of the most furious snow storms of the year. The wind rose almost to a gale. The drifting snow accumulated with incredible rapidity, and tent and pavilion were hastily abandoned by the fleeing workmen At midnight the storm was over, but our Common was a disheartening spectacle on Wednesday morning, as gangs of shovelers cleared away the drifts. While the blizzard was at its height, the driving snow had become solidly packed under the half laid floors. To remove it was impossible and the workmen's only course was to leave it there, boxed in by boards and timbers, to give an added frigidity to the wintry temperature of the tents and to freeze the feet of the thousands who trod those floors on Centennial Day. The eccentricities of the elements for the days following this blizzard might well have astonished even the hardened veterans of the weather bureau. Clouds and sunshine, mud and ice, balmy May and howling November came, one after another, in quick succession, winding up with a sharp thunder storm on the evening of the 16th, following which came the biting temperature and bitter north east wind which abated not its fury till the Centennial was over. Small wonder that the doctors reaped a golden aftermath!

One by one the arrangements for the great day were nearing completion, but, in the minds of the Committee, a misgiving at first only half acknowledged was fast growing into a definite anxiety which would not down, however much they might strive to ignore or forget it. When two historic towns were celebrating the same series of events on the same anniversary day, there needs must be some similarity in their order of procedure. Each had its orator, its procession and its dinner, with its long list of after dinner speakers. Each claimed the President of the United States and his Cabinet as special guests of honor. To obviate this trouble in some degree, the Lexington Committee had given a special prominence, on its programme, to the unveiling of the statues of Samuel Adams and John Hancock, as being a feature distinctly our own, to which our sister town could lay no claim. For four years we had worked and waited for these statues, to fill the vacant niches in Memorial Hall. Subscriptions, lecture courses and contributions of generous friends had all helped to swell the fund, and at last the requisite amount was raised and the statues were contracted for and were to be first exhibited to the public on the 19th of April.

The work, respectively, of Martin Milmore and Thomas R. Gould, they were executed, the one in Florence and the other in Rome, and, by the terms of the contracts, were each to have been delivered to the committee in Lexington on the 1st of January, 1875. Unforeseen delays had prevented the fulfillment of this agreement in either case. It was not until a week after the first of January that the Hancock statue was shipped by sailing vessel to Boston, and it was some weeks later still, when the figure of Samuel Adams was forwarded from Rome to Liverpool, whence the Cunard Company was to bring it to our shores. Newspaper items had given the statues frequent mention and their proposed unveiling had been announced on our notes of invitation. Small wonder, then, that, as the weeks passed and no statues arrived, there were anxious looks and some ominous shakes of the head among the members of the committee! The steamer leaving Liverpool on the first of April had not brought the Adams, as was positively promised. Inquiries cabled to Liverpool revealed the fact that, the ship being heavily laden, the statue had been left on the Liverpool wharf to await the sailing of the Parthia on the following week.

The disappointment of the committee was very great, and was fully shared by all our citizens. Boston had no ocean greyhound in those days. By the quickest possible run the Parthia might reach Boston on Saturday, the 17th, but incoming steamers were making long passages and reporting head winds and heavy seas, and the chances were strongly against the ship's arriving on time. The vision of the long planned Centennial with its distinctive features missing, was looming up with unpleasant vividness before the eyes of one and all.

But the fates were kinder than we knew. The good ship Parthia was staunch and strong. Buffeted by wind and wave, with great seas washing her slippery decks and a floating iceberg making a serious break in one of her watertight compartments, she still held steadily on her way, and, at two o'clock on the afternoon of Saturday, April 17th, she safely reached her dock in East Boston. It had been an anxious day in Lexington, each passing hour seemingly lessening the chances in our favor, when, shortly before three o'clock, our indefatigable fellow-townsman, Mr. George O. Davis, sent to the chairman of the Committee the following dispatch: "Steamer Parthia, with statue of Samuel Adams, just arrived. Send team to wharf immediately." That message sent eager feet flying in all directions. A special messenger, bearing an official order on the Cunard Company, caught the Boston train just as it was pulling out of the station. The express superintendent, in Boston, in his eagerness to do his whole duty, chartered a six-horse dray — when *two* horses would have served equally well — and made all speed with his imposing equipage to the Cunard wharf. By special order of the collector of the port the cargo was immediately broken open and the statue landed with all possible dispatch; and, shortly before the village clock sounded the hour of midnight, the marble presentment of our honored patriot rode majestically into Lexington, and found a resting-place on Lexington Common.

But where, meanwhile, was the companion statue? The fears of the anxious Committee were only half allayed while the figure of John Hancock was still missing.

Early in January the brig John L. Bowen, with the statue on board, had sailed from Leghorn direct for Boston. On the 28th of March she had been spoken off Bermuda, and then she disappeared from mortal ken as completely as though the seas had swallowed her. By the most liberal calculation she should have reached her port by the 9th of April, and might easily have arrived at an earlier date; but, as day after day passed and failed to bring the missing ship, all hearts grew heavy with suspense and apprehension. At last, on the morning of the 15th, a report reached us that, under stress of weather and in a somewhat disabled condition, the Bowen had sought shelter in the harbor of Vineyard Haven. In this emergency again we found a friend and active helper in the collector of the port, who immediately dispatched to Vineyard Haven the revenue cutter Gallatin, with orders to find the Bowen and tow her to Boston with all possible speed. On the morning of Friday, the 16th, the Gallatin returned, her captain reporting in person to the collector that he had been to Vineyard Haven and the Bowen was not there. "Go back and find her," was the collector's quick and decisive reply, and back the little cutter went on her blind and seemingly hopeless search. So much we knew, but, as no farther news had come to the Committee, the last gleam of hope had wellnigh faded when, late on Saturday evening, while all eyes were eagerly watching for the coming of the Adams, the following dispatch from a custom-house official told an unexpected and welcome story: "Cutter Gallatin, with brig Bowen in tow, just passing Cape Cod. Will be up at midnight. My congratulations to Committee."

I know not by what magic that brig was unloaded and the statue disembarked. I only know that, early on Sunday afternoon, just as the figure of Adams was being hoisted into its place on the platform of the pavilion, a second dray, drawn by two stalwart horses, came toiling up our village street, and a second big box was unloaded on our Common. Eager hands made quick work. The great box was hastily opened, the flannel-swathed figure was released from its wrappings, and, before we had fairly comprehended our extraordinary good fortune, our long suspense was ended, and John Hancock and Samuel Adams, in enduring marble, stood together on Lexington Green.

There was varied work done on that busy April Sunday, a day hardly less memorable, in its way, than the anniversary day which followed it. The morning had dawned on a strange and unwonted spectacle. The mammoth tents, to which the busy workmen were putting the last finishing touches, the mounds of debris which the laborers were carting away, the big baggage wagons, from which the caterer's assistants were unloading their endless supplies, and the crowds of curious lookers-on, transformed our quiet Common into a scene not easily described nor readily forgotten. There were special services in all the churches that morning, with a large and enthusiastic attendance ; but the ring of axe and hammer mingled with the sound of the church-going bell, and the babel of many voices outside the church well-nigh drowned the strains of "America" from the choir within.

Everywhere the busy decorators were at work. Perhaps it were more truthful to say they were everywhere except where they should have been ; but our judgment of those unhappy men may well be tempered with mercy. For two days they had worked untiringly, and Sunday morning still found their work sadly in arrears. With a hundred impatient people all clamoring at once, each one pressing his own individual claim to immediate attention, what wonder

Colonel Beals' assistants became confused and did some queer and startling things! When the decorations were confined to flags and bunting, and were arranged under the supervision of the Decoration Committee, they were always pleasing and often very beautiful. The uncurbed fancy of the professional decorator did not always produce the same satisfactory results. I recall one modest dwelling, then only twenty-five years old, which the workmen had conspicuously labeled "Birthplace of American Liberty," and surmounted this remarkable legend with a lifesized, full-length portrait of George Washington! "Only that and nothing more." When the aggrieved owner ventured a meek remonstrance against such a very unsuitable design, the astonished decorator, with an impressive stare, replied: "I *thought* I was making this house *A 1*."

But the busiest day must end at last, and, while still the workman sawed and hammered, while the anxious Committee still hurried to and fro, while the long procession of carriages and foot passengers still moved slowly up and down our streets, night came, dreary, cold and overcast, with a howling northeast wind and a threatening outlook for the morrow. The evening religious service, in the town hall, with its distinguished speakers and its elaborate musical programme, could but partially offset the extremely unsabbath-like character of that memorable Sunday.

It is not my purpose to attempt any history of the Centennial Day itself. We all remember it, and the personal experiences of the participants have been many times recounted, and have lost nothing in the repetition In its important features the day was a complete and memorable success. To us who remember the details, and know how the elements and the unprecedented crowds combined to overturn all the calculations of our careful Committee, the grotesque incidents which marked the Centennial must ever be a source of mingled amusement and regret. No mouse ever saw his well-laid plans going more hopelessly agley! The crowded trains that wouldn't move, the impatient guests who couldn't arrive, the officials who clung desperately to the lowest steps of overfilled omnibuses instead of reclining in luxurious carriages prepared for their occupancy, the great procession which "dragged its slow length along" through the surging crowds which blocked every foot of its way, the hungry mobs that raided private larders and invaded the most sacred precincts of our homes, and the bleak, cold wind which howled round great and small alike, — these are some of the memories of that long-planned, long-talked-of Centennial Day.

I will not weary you with the particulars, but I cannot forbear a passing mention of those who were our guests that day. Of the many committees which had toiled through that long winter of preparation, perhaps the Invitation Committee had been deepest in work and worry, for on those three individuals fell the duty of gathering, from far and near, the distinguished men who should do honor to the day. How thorough was their work and how widely those notes of invitation flew over the length and breadth of the land, the great array of guests who thronged our pavilion bore ample testimony. I think our citizens have never fully realized the distinguished company which gathered here that day. We all remember the invading host which, *uninvited*, took possession of our town; but to the real guests of honor some of us have given little thought. Governors, congressmen, judges and professional men were "thick as autumnal leaves that strew the brooks in Vallombrosa;" but there were other guests that day whose noble words and golden deeds will live when official rank is long forgotten. On that flag-draped platform were men eminent in science, in letters and in philanthropy. There were men whose halting step or empty sleeve told of patriotic blood freely shed in their country's cause; and not unmeet it seemed that with the war-worn soldier there should come the venerable author of "America" and the noble woman to whose inspired pen we owe "The Battle Hymn of the Republic." President Grant and his Cabinet came late. How that distinguished soldier effected his retreat from Concord that day, by what military manœuvre he made his forced march on Lexington, has never, I think, been satisfactorily explained. Some said he came in an omnibus. There were rumors of other vehicles, more or less stately in character, which were successively pressed into his service. He certainly was not in the railway train which stood stalled for hours on the wind-swept meadows near North Lexington, and in which certain members of the Reception Committee spent a good portion of their day. In some way unknown to history, by back roads or cross roads, avoiding the surging crowds which blocked the historic highway between Lexington and Concord, late but undaunted, the President and his Cabinet appeared at last, and occupied an honored place in our procession, our dinner tent and at our evening reception. Secretary Robeson was, unfortunately, lost in transit and, reaching Lexington somewhat later than his chief, experienced some difficulty in proving his identity to the suspicious policemen on duty at the tents. In vain he assured them that the head of the Navy Department stood before them. A blue-coated guardian of the peace sniffed contemptuously as he made reply: "That won't do! We have had too many secretaries round here to-day already." Very pleasant to the eye of the perturbed Cabinet minister was the passing member of the Reception Committee who rescued him from his undignified dilemma.

It was too cold and inclement a day for the social amenities to be very rigorously observed, either by policemen or by guests, and some amusing breaches of decorum were the direct result. There remains photographed on my memory the picture of a white-haired doctor of divinity surreptitiously and unlawfully holding up the flap of the dinner tent while a grave and dignified professor of the Harvard Law School did gracefully crawl under.

But, with the many distinguished men whom we gladly welcomed to our midst that day, there came one little woman from New Jersey, whose antecedents gave her a claim upon our hospitality, and whose personal characteristics seem worthy of remembrance. Few of our people even heard her name. Still fewer met her face to face. It was my privilege, through letters and through repeated interviews, to know her, for a short period, somewhat familiarly, and perhaps I cannot better close these rambling memories than by briefly sketching the quaint little body who was for four days our guest.

Early in the year a citizen of a neighboring town had called the attention of the Committee to Miss Sarah Smith Stafford of Trenton, New Jersey, who, as a descendant of famous Revolutionary ancestors and as possessor of numerous Revolutionary relics, seemed entitled to recognition from Lexington. A somewhat voluminous correspondence with Miss Stafford brought out some interesting facts regarding herself, her ancestors and her possessions,—facts which I briefly give as nearly as possible in the order in which she gave them to me.

Fully to understand Miss Stafford's antecedents, it is necessary to go back to the first days of September, 1779, when the American armed ship Kitty, commanded by Capt. Philip Stafford, was seized by a British Man-of-War and all on board were put in irons. On the 13th of September Commodore Paul Jones, commanding the American ship Bon Homme Richard, captured the Man-of-War and her prize, liberated the prisoners and ironed their English captors. Serving on the Kitty was Captain Stafford's young nephew, James Bayard Stafford, a young man who by education and training was somewhat superior to his brother sailors; and when the entire crew volunteered to serve on the ship which had rescued them, young Stafford was given a lieutenant's command. Thus it came to pass that he served as a volunteer officer under Paul Jones in the engagement between the Bon Homme Richard and the Serapis, on the 23d of September, 1779. When the Richard went into action there floated from her masthead a little flag, less than four yards in length, for which was claimed the proud distinction of being the first flag bearing the stars and stripes ever carried by an American warship and the first ever saluted by a foreign naval power.

When the battle was at its height this flag was shot away and must have been lost past recovery but for the prompt action of the young volunteer, Lieutenant Stafford, who at the risk of his life sprang over the ship's side, rescued the flag and brought it safely back on board. While replacing it at the masthead he received a severe and painful wound from which he never ceased to suffer. When the ship went down, almost in the hour of victory, Paul Jones transferred the precious flag to the American ship Alliance, where it remained till the close of the Revolution, when it came into the possession of the Marine Committee. Rallying from his serious wounds, Lieutenant Stafford served through the war, doing valiant service wherever duty called him, and after the return of peace the Marine Committee, which was, I suppose, the modest forerunner of our Navy Department, presented to the brave officer the flag he had rescued, then and now known as the flag of Paul Jones. After the close of the war, Lieutenant Stafford married a brave Massachusetts woman, two of whose relatives had fallen on the 19th of April, at Menotomy, and her father later at White Plains. Of the little family reared in their New Jersey home, Sarah Smith Stafford was the only daughter and, perhaps, the youngest child. With this double inheritance of Revolutionary blood and reared in an atmosphere of Revolutionary tradition, patriotism became a religion in the mind of the little girl. Idolizing her invalid father, she loved with almost equal devotion the country for which his blood was shed, and the "flag of Paul Jones," the visible emblem of that country's glory and that father's valor, became a sacred possession in her childish eyes. When, at last, the father and mother vanished from the little home, perhaps it is not strange that the lonely daughter grew into a woman of one idea, developing some attendant eccentricities. Her home, for many years, was on the battlefield of Trenton. One who visited her there says it was a museum of Revolutionary relics. The outbreak of our Civil War found Miss Stafford one of the most zealous workers in the Union cause. Her little fortune of $12,000 she immediately loaned without security to the State of New Jersey, to aid in equipping the first New Jersey Volunteers, simply replying to the remonstrances of cautious friends, "What is money, if you have no country?"

In 1849 her widowed mother had made application to Congress for renumeration for her husband's services on the Bon Homme Richard, but there were legal technicalities

in the way, and for many years the matter was allowed to
drop. In 1872 the daughter renewed the application. Before it had been acted upon by Congress, the news reached
Washington one morning of the robbing of the Trenton
Bank and the total loss of all Miss Stafford's property deposited therein. The New Jersey senators lost no time in
bringing the matter forward. In the Congressional Record
of that year I find a full report of the glowing tributes to
the services of Lieutenant Stafford, and of the promptness
with which, then and there, ninety-three years after those
services were rendered, Congress, without a dissenting
voice, voted $8,000 back pay to the brave Lieutenant's
daughter.

And this was the little woman who was Lexington's
guest on Centennial Day, and the flag she brought, the
flag of Paul Jones, was the historic piece of bunting which
held the place of honor among our platform decorations,
between the palmetto and the pine, and which has been
recently presented to President McKinley for deposit in
tho National Museum. In consideration of her age and
presumable infirmities, the invitation extended to Miss
Stafford had been a very generous one, and she came to us
on Friday, April 16, and left on the afternoon of Tuesday,
the 20th.

Perhaps the prospect of a four days' visit with a voluble
old lady seemed a little overwhelming to the gentlemen of
the Invitation Committee. Certain it is that the services
of the Committee's feminine attaché were again put in requi-
sition, and to her watchful care the visitor was committed.
We looked for a fragile, delicate, infirm old lady, but there
came to us a rotund, erect little body, with white hair and
wrinkled visage, it is true, but with an unconquerable
sprightliness of manner and a step as springing as a girl's.

Entire indifference to fashion's mandate was written on every detail of her quaint costume. She was laboriously handling a monstrous bag of divers hues when I met her at the station. Its proportions and its weight were almost too much for her slender strength, but the flag, the precious flag, was hidden within its vast recesses and no persuasions could induce her to trust it to my care. The other relics she was to exhibit here had come to us by express, but to no vandal hand would she intrust the most treasured possession of them all, and she climbed into the waiting carriage still clutching with unyielding grip the receptacle which contained her priceless flag.

During the days which followed, our interviews were many and sometimes extended, and I am not sure the Committee were not wise in entertaining her by proxy. Her interest in the approaching celebration never flagged, but the courage with which she faced the discomforts of that trying day was something we were quite unable to foresee. Remembering that Centennial morning, with its wintry temperature and its biting wind, our surprise may be imagined when Miss Stafford presented herself, waiting to be escorted to her place in the pavilion. She wore a black silk gown of good material but ancient cut, a white shawl of medium weight, and on her silver locks there rested simply a white muslin cap with flying streamers. Her wrinkled face was blue with cold, which all the fires of patriotism could not wholly overcome, but her eye was as bright and her manner as vivacious as ever. In vain we protested against such an unsuitable attire on such a freezing day. 'Twas throwing words away. She assured us that the shawl was the proper thing to wear and the cap was her Centennial Cap, and wear them she would in spite of wind and weather; and wear them she did through all that bitter day.

The crowds were already upon our streets, but through the mass of patriotic humanity this resolute little body, with flying cap strings and fluttering shawl, was escorted to her assigned place in the pavilion. Late in the afternoon, when cold and fatigue had driven the guests by hundreds from the dinner tent, and when the brave men who remained were turning their ulster collars up around their ears, I saw the plucky woman with her white shawl drawn up over her head and pinned securely under her quivering chin, thus adding very materially to the general picturesqueness of her appearance, but very little, I fear, to her bodily comfort. So much, and no more, this valiant Daughter of the Revolution yielded to the weather!

Late in the afternoon of Tuesday, April 20, we saw Miss Stafford off on her homeward way, and after that we saw her face no more. One or two enthusiastic letters came back to us from her New Jersey home. Occasionally the newspapers recorded her presence at some patriotic gathering. She took her beloved flag to the opening of the Philadelphia Centennial, and was an honored guest during her stay. But the infirmities of age were coming fast, however resolutely she might resist their approach. It was not long before we read, one morning, that the end had come. Worn out at last, the tired body was laid to rest beside its kindred dust, and at her own request she was carried to her grave with the flag of Paul Jones draped upon her casket.

May we all be as loyal as she to the country that flag represents!

RECOLLECTIONS OF THE THIRD MEETING-HOUSE IN LEXINGTON, ERECTED 1794.

BY FRANCIS BROWN. READ OCTOBER 8, 1901.

In these recollections of the Lexington Meeting-house, I shall omit the oldest structures and confine myself to the one erected in 1794, which was my only place of public worship in the town.

It was a large two-story wooden building, located a few feet north of the historical-memorial block or pulpit recently stationed on the southerly angle of the Common. It was a building of very modest style and form, and its dimensions were, I think, about eighty by fifty feet. It had a porch at the front about twenty-five by twenty feet, opening to the main building, with a façade over the door, on which was painted in black figures "1794."

Although not standing on any marked elevation, the house was found, by an engineer, to occupy a level ninety feet above the foundation of the church at Concord. Incredible as this may appear, it is doubtless true, as not less than five streams originating in Lexington are found running out of the town in different directions,— into the Concord, Mystic and Merrimac rivers,— showing plainly, by its elevation, affecting air and drainage, why Lexington is remarkably healthful and pleasant.

Let us now look at the interior of the Meeting-House. The lower floor was nearly covered with square pews, one range extending by the windows entirely round from one side of the pulpit to the other, and called the wall-pews, with an aisle just within the circuit. One third of the central area was used for slips for the aged, partially deaf, etc., the different sexes occupying separately the right and left side, and the other two-thirds of the center were occupied for pews.

A range of gallery extended along the front as well as both the ends, with a line of square pews by the windows. The front portion of the front gallery was occupied by the singers, while the end galleries were set apart for the second grade of adults of both sexes, a few disorderly boys with a tything-man or two to preserve order, and in one corner a few relics of law-regulated slavery, under the names of Cæsar Mason, Betsy Tulip, Charity Bridge and Dinah Lawrence.

And here a few words respecting the pulpit, which was in those days considered a place of so much sacredness that few save the authorized ones had courage to enter it. It was made of pine and painted white, with access given to it by a flight of six or seven steps on each side, a large window in its rear, a red or maroon colored Bible cushion, a black Bible and a black hymn book of the Tate and Brady collection I think.

Overhead hung, suspended by an iron rod, a "sounding-board," circular in form, coming down to within twelve or eighteen inches of the minister's head; and this, I well remember, frequently disturbed my juvenile apprehension, lest it might fall upon and crush the poor preacher below. Here let me note that I once saw a dove come in at an open window and light upon the sounding-board and there sit for a while, bobbing his head and peeping over the edge of the board on the heads of his fellow-worshipers below, very much amusing the juveniles and puzzling the pastor to know what the matter could be.

In this connection let us say a word about the preaching.

As there was but one church in the town, we had but one prevailing sentiment to cherish, one cluster of dogmas to examine and one conclusion, set forth, to arrive at; so we had little to excite discussion, and we patiently took what was given us and waited, wished and wondered, according to our peculiar circumstances. One thing I ought to acknowledge, however; we had very long discourses, often requiring a full hour in their delivery, and sometimes an hour and a half; two of them surely on each Sunday, so that if any fell short in quality it was made up and presented in quantity.

In connection with this, let us call up the subject of music. As often as once in two or three years the town would vote a sum of money sufficient to secure a teacher of singing, and although the cost was incurred for the benefit of the parish, it was by law made a town charge. Seasonable notice would be given of the opening of the school and all were invited to attend. Fifty, or perhaps one hundred, would appear, candle in hand, as required. Sounding of individual voices and trials to discover individual taste and talent, by the teacher, would occupy two or three of the earliest sessions of the school, and the result of the inquiries would generally be that about half the number of attendants would be kindly advised not to incur the expense of a tune-book. The balance, however, was always found sufficient to fill the singers' seats in the church and with instrumental aid such as was afforded by the bass-viol, French horn, bassoon, violin, clarinet and flute, with the help of a tuning-fork, after about six or eight weeks of training, the choir was qualified and willing to meet the public expectations.

As regards the heating of the premises, there was no furnace, stove, steam or anything else to soften the arctic temperature of the house during the wintry season excepting a few foot-stoves brought by ladies who came in their sleighs from distant homes. To all other persons the state of the atmosphere was anything but agreeable or tolerable during a two-hours' sitting. But time works wonders, it is truly said, and finally one appeared here in the form of a large wood-stove, placed near the head of the broad aisle, directly in front of the pulpit, the smoke-pipe rising ten or twelve feet and branching off to each end of the building, out underneath the galleries. This inaugurated the warming process for church comfort. May science and art continue to invent and improve plans for securing its more perfect accomplishment!

The old church had three outside entrances. That one looking down the main street led through the porch directly into the church and by a side stairway to the gallery. The west end also opened a way into the church below and through a double stairway into the gallery. The east end had a projection, including a belfry, sixty or seventy feet high, which sustained a steeple of about as much added height. On the steeple's pinnacle, a weather-vane, of the semblance of a rooster, swung for many years, doing its duty faithfully, until, on an exceedingly cold, dark and tempestuous evening, a flock of wild geese, almost exhausted, on their way homeward, making a great noise, settled down too low for safety, till one of their number came in contact with the rooster's tail and bent it around to a right angle; but the contact proved fatal to the goose, it being found dead in the morning at the base of the belfry. A way was opened through this porch into the church, again by a double staircase to the gallery, and thence by a single flight of steps to the belfry or bell-deck, where the thoughtless boy would sometimes stray on a "Sunday noon," and, ignorant or forgetful of the "first afternoon ringing," would find himself surprised and astounded with the noise when too late to retreat.

I remember being told by my father, who was generally correct on such matters, that, when the four corner-posts of this belfry were raised, the machinery was so arranged that to each separate post, at the end which went uppermost, a man with a strip of board, a hammer and some nails was lashed, and when the posts were raised to a perpendicular position each man coöperated with his neighbor on his right and left hand, by nailing together the ends of the several posts, thus completing the object of their daring exploit. Three of these men, by the means prepared for their descent, were lowered down, when the fourth one, a sailor, still aloft, rose and walked around from post to post, on the edge of the strips of board, and then descended, applauded by many for his success and denounced for his foolhardiness by the wiser ones standing awe-struck below. The bell of the church was very high-keyed and its tone was easily distinguished from the neighboring town bells when rung for fires. It had, however, one substantial quality. When the next bell was contracted for, the founder preferred, rather than to lower the old bell by derrick, to plunge it from the bell-deck and take his chances of breaking it. It fell and struck the hard road without a crack or scar.

Our old church had neither blinds, shades, shutters nor curtains, no carpets, seat-cushions, organ or library, no chapel, Sunday-school room or horse-shed, no pictures or sacred relics save the old red morocco-covered Bible in the pulpit, bearing upon its fly-leaf the gift-token to the parish in the familiar handwriting of Governor John Hancock.

Thus, without ornament, convenience or comfort, we loved

and honored the old meeting-house and approached it nearly every Sabbath day, riding and even walking one, two or three miles to do it and we left it feeling that it was good for us that we had met the demand and that we had gained something to aid us in the formation of religious character.

We had no special religious instruction suited to the growth or culture of the young mind, excepting, if it could be so considered, when the minister came into the secular schoolroom, two or three times during the school season, on a Saturday afternonoon and "catechised" us from the famous New England Primer. The only thing pleasant or profitable to me in this connection, which I now remember, is the fact that Mr. Williams, on one of his visits, gave me a "fourpence halfpenny piece" for proficiency in the catechism exercise when a pupil of four or five years.

There is another subject, in this connection, which must not be passed without due notice. I refer to the clergymen who filled our pulpit and honored their profession at the time we are considering, viz., Mr. Clarke, Mr. Williams and Mr. Briggs. Although I do not press the claim of friendly relationship to the first named, yet, as he was the only religious guide and teacher of the town, and as my birthday occurred about three years before his decease, I conclude that he made many calls at the home of my parents, and that I was as often awed into silence by the wonderful presence; and I can now almost feel his gentle hand patting my head and hear his kind word, full of religious instruction on filial, fraternal and religious duties. So I can claim him, as he was, as my first pastor; and, since he was both immediately before and after his death so much a theme of conversation with my parents and their neighbors, it is no wonder that his impress of character was deeply fixed in my memory.

He was a good pastor and he was a statesman worthy of all praise, honor and imitation. In our terrible Revolutionary struggle he was among the earliest, purest and most fearless advocates of freedom. In thought, word and deed he "nobly dared to be free." Has his memory been justly appreciated and honored, and has his name filled the place deserved by it on the roll of fame? Many times I have thought it was not so. Historians should look to this.

He was a good citizen, leader, counselor and friend. Whenever his influence prevailed, there was no need of police court or police officers. If Smith and Jones came to any war of words more or less angry, upon agreement to refer the matter to Parson Clarke the scene at once brightened and the storm-cloud was sure to be dispelled. The contestants came and related and argued, and the decision was quick and final. "Jones, your bull is a burly and dangerous animal and should be shut up in barn or barnyard; and, Smith, if your fences had been kept in better order, your ox would not have been gored. Go, both of you, and do your duty, and shake hands as friends," and this was sure to be done.

In his domestic relations he was exemplary; a little stern, perhaps some would say, but a tree should be judged by its fruits, and as he sent out into the world's active and worthy service six sons and six daughters, no one would fail to acknowledge the genuineness of his family government in securing filial love and obedience. I recollect hearing the following specimen of his training.

Young folks of that day, as now, were apt to be sleepy in the morning, and prone to ignore the early call to arise. This could not be allowed by the parson, and he would, as he had occasion, go to the foot of the stairway and, aloud, give the peculiar word of command, viz.: —

"Polly, Betsey, Lydia,
Lucy, Patty, Sally,
Thomas, Jonas, William,
Peter, Bowen, Harry,
GET UP!"

and it was added that, before the roll-call was concluded, every foot had reached the floor, and every ear was saluted with the military words, "Right! Dress!"

There stands out, on my memorial tablet, Avery Williams, a man of less than middle age, slender of figure and of rather gloomy aspect, seemingly full of thought, — uncongenial thought, — and, withal, reluctant to entertain cheerfulness or smiles in his musings or conversation. He was not of the practical turn of his predecessor, either in mind or manner, and was very unlike him. A scholar, perhaps, but not well acquainted with human nature, and not fitted to fill the vacancy that had existed in the parish. He was blind to the needs of his people, and then unyielding to the circumstances by which he was attended. He was a decided follower of John Calvin, and allowed no other doctrines than those he entertained to be true. He was also, in politics, a strong and ardent Federalist, and as the War of 1812 was taking form and direction, and as opinions were ripening into the most violent manifestations at this time, the town being decidedly Republican in politics, and, withal, liberal in its religious tone and character, conversation soon resulted in struggle, and unwise words uttered in the pulpit, and misunderstood and misjudged in the pews, brought about a condition of things tending to create bad feeling between pastor and people. An instance of outbreak may be cited as in point.

It was customary on Thanksgiving Day to have some

special piece of music sung by the choir at the close of divine service. On this special occasion the singers had made choice of the "Ode on Science," which contains some sentences decidedly offensive to the Federal or British politician. The clouds of strife were at once seen rising and threatening a storm. The hint was immediately afloat that the minister would neither read the ode nor give opportunity for its use. The chorister had seasonable notice of what would probably occur, and marshalled his forces to meet the worst. So, after the short prayer, *at once* an attempt was made to pronounce the benediction, but in an instant the gallery was alive with tumultuous song. Every voice and every instrument was urged to give its variety and tone to the combination, and it seemed as if the roof would be raised by the effort. I heard the leader declare, aloud, as soon as he came outside the church door, that "if the minister would not *read* it, he should *hear* it with a vengeance." Soon after this the ministry of Mr. Williams was ended. Doubtless wrong existed on both sides. It generally does in such cases.

I was personally present when Mr. Williams christened the oldest five of the children of my parents, a fact I respectfully desire to remember.

We come, next, to the ministry of the Rev. Charles Briggs. He was, I think, a graduate of the Harvard Divinity School.

About four years after Mr. Williams left the parish, and after quite a number of candidates of different denominations had been listened to, the church and congregation came, quite unanimously, to the choice of Mr. Briggs in the year 1819. He was comparatively young, and fresh from the schools, but he ripened rapidly into favor with his people. He was a genial, wise and kind man, an acceptable teacher, exemplar and friend. I knew him well. I loved him much. I remember many of his terse and valuable sentences, both in the pulpit and in private intercourse, containing thoughts always bearing with good and enduring effect upon the life and character of those who heard him, and especially upon the young listener. He was quite popular when I left the town.

In connection with the church organization, I must next introduce the *deacons* of the parish; for, in those early times, the office was one of much dignity and importance, and we young folks were taught to regard the deacons as worthy of all honor and respect. My earliest recollections bring up but two, James Brown and Isaac Hastings, owners of pews at the extreme northeast and northwest angles of the lower floor of the house. But, personally and officially, they filled other and more distinguished seats, at the foot of the pulpit stairs, their chairs standing at each end of the communion table and facing the audience. Why they were so stationed I, as a little fellow, was much puzzled to know; whether because they were good-looking men, whether because they were exemplary men, or whether to regulate the conduct of such as could not appreciate the service; and I, as yet, remain unenlightened. It was once their duty to "line the hymns" to be intoned by the choir, and I believe I have witnessed the exercise in our church, but cannot feel quite sure of it, as the practice was discontinued about the time alluded to.

I cannot refrain from noticing briefly a few of the prevalent customs of the date and locality we are describing.

Then, as now, young folks were in the habit of forming matrimonial engagements. Then, as now, legal notice of marriage intentions must be publicly given, and, instead of procuring a certificate of such notice, as now practiced, the town clerk, as directed, would rise in his pew, immediately after the benediction, at the close of the afternoon service, and, with stentorian voice, would declare that "marriage is intended between A. B. of Lexington and C. D. of Concord, or E. F. and G. H., both of Lexington." This had to be repeated two succeeding Sabbaths to meet the demands of the law. Once, I remember well, it proved quite an amusing occurrence to us. The town clerk, finding himself a very much interested party to the notice, nothing daunted, rose and manfully showed himself equal to the occasion, as, with full voice, he published his own bann s to our entire satisfaction. Another mode of making public these intentions was to nail upon the church door a public declaration of the facts in the case.

Another prevailing custom of the time was that, if a death occurred in any family of the parish, "a note was put up" (as it was expressed) by the nearest of kin, asking that the Disposer of events would convert the bereavement into a blessing of "spiritual and everlasting good" to the mourning relatives.

If a member of the family was about to start on a *long journey*, — to *Hartford* or *New York*, — it was customary for friends to ask, in this public manner, for the protecting care of the Good Spirit, for its wise guidance and for the speedy return of the wanderer to his home and family. Again, when a family of the parish was blest by the birth of a child, it was deemed a joy and a duty to ask for the sympathy of friends, to join in a prayer of thankfulness to God for "mercies received." Scarcely a Sabbath passed that some one or more of such papers were not read before the prayer, and often became a dominant feature of the invocation. Newspapers, then, were very scarce, and news of a local character moved slowly and doubtfully, and the intelligence these offerings gave was prized and borne away to the several homes with the satisfaction of having news from headquarters.

I distinctly recollect the old horse-block, located about twenty feet from the southeast corner of the building. It was made of hewn granite blocks, laid about four feet by four and three feet high, with three steps leading to the top. At that time there were very few carriages, excepting wagons, in use in the town, and many single and double horseloads of church-goers were seen, on Sundays, approaching the house of worship with a man astride in front, and, behind him, on a pillion, his wife, and sometimes, in her lap, a babe. The horse was guided up to the side of the block, and the animal unburthened by the party or their friends.

I trust I may be allowed to add a short anecdote here in connection with this old block. My father many times told me that, when a lad, one Sunday noontime he happened to be sitting on the block, and overheard two antiquated dames discussing the profound subjects of life, death and the judgment day. They looked painfully puzzled, anxious and dissatisfied with the teachings of the pulpit and the evidences of the Scriptures, till, finally, they became partially exhausted and quieted.

The silence was at last broken by the following query and answer:

"Aunt Patty, what do you really believe on this dreadful subject?"

The answer at last came in long-drawn and subdued sentences and sighs:

"Sister, I dont know what to say. *Sometimes I think, and then — again — I don't know.*"

The lad was amused and told it to his generation. I pass it along to mine.

A few words now about the trees. Immediately about the church there was but little foliage. Two or three trees of a leafless look had grown up at the rear of the building, nearly behind the pulpit. Beside these there was but a single one that ornamented the immediate surroundings. This tree was a stately elm which stood at the southeast corner of the building, midway between the belfry and horse-block. Neither of the trees, however, was so situated as to afford shade or shelter over man or animal. A range of posts, about twenty feet from the front of the house, was set, beginning at the front porch and extending, in each direction, to the corners, right and left. These posts were connected at the top by a rail to which the horses were tied, and where they stood, uncovered, without shed, shade or blanket to protect them from the sun, storm or flies during the services in church.

In the old Merriam House (Buckman Tavern) now standing is said to have been located the first post-office of the town. I remember having gone there for letters when the business of the office was transacted in a small building, now standing, at the northeast corner of the house.

The Town Library, consisting of from one hundred to two hundred volumes, during the period of which I am writing, was kept, successively, at the houses of Rufus Merriam, Nathan Munroe and Joshua Russell. The collection, I think, was composed chiefly of books of History and Travels, a few Biographies and Moral Essays, together with a scanty supply of Poetry, with here and there a volume on Art, Science and Natural History.

THE EPITAPHS IN THE BURYING-GROUNDS AT LEXINGTON, MASS.

READ BY FRANCIS H. BROWN, M.D., OCTOBER 14, 1902.

During the summer months of 1901-02 it was my privilege to pass a certain time in the Town of Lexington, where many of my ancestors were born, and have lived and died.

I was led to carry out a plan which had for some time been in my mind, to study the records of the early and the later town-folk, in that form which may be said to be contemporaneous with them, and so substantially correct. A gravestone tells the truth! Yes, presumably so, so far as dates are concerned; and, to that extent, it is a valuable aid in the study of the history and the biography of the people of the town. In that view I trust I may have done a service by copying some 716 epitaphs. With all the quaintness of diction, the peculiarities of spelling, of punctuation and of type, they are accurate transcripts from the stones, and may be considered as correct biographical records as those of the family Bibles of the inhabitants of this community.

Hidden behind the records which we gather from the headstones, how much of family history lies concealed!— of strenuous life; of struggles of the husbandmen in the meadows and fields; of the going back and forth, in the roads and byways of the town; of the holding of offices of honor and trust as selectmen, assessors and treasurers, enjoying the confidence of fellow-townsmen; of proving themselves good, honest, trustworthy New England people. The circumstances of these lives are a precious inheritance to those who can claim them as those of ancestors.

A copy of these epitaphs accompanies this paper, and will be deposited, with it, in the archives of the Lexington Historical Society. Moreover, I have made, in connection with the epitaphs, footnotes giving the line of ancestry and many biographical memoranda concerning a considerable number of the decedents. Still farther, I am able to exhibit lithographic copies of plans of the old burying-ground and the Robbins Cemetery, in which the gravestones, as to-day situated, are carefully marked and numbered. The transcript of the epitaph gives, with each one, a number which will serve to indicate the locality of each grave. The plans referred to have been made with much care and great labor by Mr. Eli M. Robbins, a native of the town and now a resident. For permission to use them and for valuable assistance in preparing this paper I am indebted to him.

Another copy of this paper and of the accompanying epitaphs will be placed in the Library of the New England Historic-Genealogical Society in Boston.

I think I may be pardoned if I express the regret that many of the dates on the gravestones do not entirely conform with the printed records in the History of the town; that the gravestones, many of them, have been removed from the actual places of burial, and that the presumption is strong that many stones, which would give us valuable information concerning early inhabitants, are buried beneath the sod, or have furnished useful — but unsentimental — adjuvants to stone walls, the foundations of buildings or the covering of drains. You will excuse the plain language. I speak as a historian and one dealing with facts. I trust that some of the missing stones may be recovered in due time.

It is very reasonable to suppose, and indeed Mr. Robbins bears me out in the suggestion, that *all* parts of the old burying-ground now wanting stones are thickly populated with the remains of those whose stones are set up in serried lines or have been destroyed or buried.

Within a few years Mr. Henry A. May of Roxbury, a professional genealogist, suggested to his kinsman, Mr. John James May of Dorchester, a member of the New England Historic-Genealogical Society, the necessity of "taking off the epitaphs" in the various burying-grounds throughout the State, in order that records, supposed to be of unfailing accuracy, on stones, slowly but surely yielding to the ravages of time, might be preserved for the benefit of future genealogists and historians. The suggestion was at once accepted by Mr. J. J. May, and he was appointed by the Society the chairman of a committee to carry out the plan.

The plan of Mr. H. A. May was that a central and organized body, like the Historic Genealogical Society, should enlist the interest of the inhabitants in every town in the Commonwealth, with the request that persons in the various towns, with historical interest and local pride, should take the matter in hand, and that complete lists, so far as possible, should be made of decedents in the towns as shown by the memorial stones. The town clerk of Lexington was asked to interest himself in this plan, and he called it to the attention of Miss Sarah Eddy Holmes. To her the author of this paper is much indebted for valuable assistance in its preparation.

It is interesting, in this connection, to refer in a few words to the earliest history of this town, as it has been laboriously and, I am sure, accurately set down by the Rev. Carleton A. Staples, the warm-hearted, earnest Christian minister of the First Parish.

Did it ever occur to you, who live in Lexington in 1902, to recall your ancestors, those who in 1638 came out here to the Cambridge Farms, into the wilderness, from the little town of Boston and Watertown? Do you realize how quaint they were in their dress and their speech, and how stern in their religion and their forms of daily life; how they put forth their muscle and their brawn to wrest from nature the treasures which she held bound up in the woods and the fields and the meadows of the town?

It is a matter of history and of evolution, if it may so be called, to note how the course of the town went on, as that of all our towns has done; with allegiance to the king and the royal government; how the people took part in the Indian wars, and how Hugh Mason and John Mason and the others were in the Narragansett war; how Edmund Munroe and his kinsmen went off with the Roger's Rangers, and spared not their lives at Ticonderoga and Lake George; how Parson Clarke harbored in his home Hancock and Adams, and there, at that time, wrote philippics which were strongholds for the men of Middlesex County. Do you recall that here, on Lexington Common, the first actual resistance to British control took place, by which I mean that the spirit of the English men, who came to this country in 1620 and 1630, filled with the spirit of Magna Charta, would not be satisfied except with every liberty which the principles of their birthright could furnish?

If it be true that Herlackenden came, personally or by proxy, to this neighborhood in 1638 and died in the same year, and if Pelham came about that year and soon married the widow of Herlackenden, holding many acres of ground in the centre of the town, with only one house until the Pelham family sold to Muzzey in 1693;—these facts would imply a very small clientele within the limits of the up-in-town village from which to draw denizens for the ancient burying-ground. But Mr. Staples tells us there were forty houses and two hundred inhabitants in the town in 1693, and, while the centre was held as a large manor property, there were many outlying farms and holdings which were brought into the limits of the newly incorporated town in 1713. Such an analysis seems needed as a preliminary to the question, " Who ought to have been laid in our burying-ground ? "

It is natural to suppose that, with the earliest conditions of the population of our country towns, the dead were buried on the farms, at least till the parish, the church and the public burying-ground were established ; but no evidences of such burials, by headstones or otherwise, are known to-day. At the same time we do not know that the burying-grounds are not as old as the settlements. The stones are no certain guide to the age of graveyards.

I have been told that, besides the old burying-ground, the burials beneath the battle monument, the Robbins cemetery in the East Village and the new cemetery, there are no known places of sepulture in our town.

Since writing this I learn that a tomb was built on the Reuben Reed place on the Lowell turnpike, and that it may still be there ; also that the bodies of some who were buried on the Nathaniel Pierce place were removed some years ago to the new cemetery.

I find that in 1692 John Munroe gave the town a plot of land for a burying-ground ; he was the son of the immigrant William, and himself the father of ten children by his wife Hannah ; he was a subscriber to the meeting-house, and filled many offices in the gift of the town ; he was employed many years to ring the bell and " sweep out the meeting-house," and was finally gathered to his fathers in 1753. This plot of land is the northwest portion of the present ground ; its northern limit corresponds to a line drawn in front of the four tombs at the right of the present entrance avenue, and is continued to the back wall. This limit is the northern boundary of the Munroe land and the southern limit of the Pelham property.

In 1747 the ground was enlarged by purchase of land from William Munroe, "the blacksmith" (1701-1783), by a committee of which William Munroe (1703-1747) was the chairman. You all know the account of his getting cold while haying in his meadow, and that he was the first buried in this portion of the ground.

In 1811 a plot of land was bought just outside the passage to the old ground on the Pelham, land and on this four tombs were built, which bear the names of Harrington, Augustus, Munroe and Fessenden.

Three of the name of Jonathan Harrington were present at the Battle of Lexington. Jonathan Harrington married Ruth Fiske, was wounded on the battlefield, dragged himself to his own doorstep now on Elm Avenue, and died in the presence of his wife. Jonathan Harrington, b. May 21, 1723, d. 1809, mar. Widow Abigail Dunster. His daughter Rebecca married Edmund Munroe in 1769, who was killed at Monmouth in 1778. His son, Jonathan, the fifer of the minute-men and the last survivor of the Battle of Lexington, is buried with him in the same tomb.

Later an additional lot of land was bought by various residents of the town, to the north of the four tombs and extending to the northeast limit. It is known as the Proprietor's Lot. A list of those buried in this plot is given with the copy deposited with the Historic-Genealogical Society.

Still later a lot of land was set aside by members of the Robbins and Simonds families. A lithograph of this portion of the burying-ground, from a drawing of Mr. Eli M. Robbins, accompanies this paper.

The private burying-ground of the Robbins family in the East Village was established by Stephen Robbins (1758–1847). Twenty-one epitaphs are now found in this yard; but it is well known that some hundred persons have been buried there. A complete list was given by Caira Robbins to her nephew, Eli M. Robbins, and this was copied by him and placed in one of the record books of the town. It has now been copied by Miss Holmes and is incorporated with this paper.

It is interesting to note the oldest known stones in the town.

Daniel Tedd (Tidd) died November 29, 1690. This is the oldest stone which we find to-day.

Isaac Stone died December 10, 1690.

Lydia Meriam, December 29, 1690.

Mary, wife of Joseph Teed, and Rachel, daughter of John and Rachel Stone died August 31, 1692.

"Sacred to Liberty and the rights of mankind." Certainly no mortuary record of the town of Lexington would be complete which did not recall the names on the battle monument on the village green.

"Ensign Robert Munroe, Jonas Parker, Samuel Hadley, Jonathan Harrington, Jr., Isaac Muzzey, Caleb Harrington, John Brown, Asahel Porter of Woburn" fell on that day, the first victims to the sword of British tyranny and oppression," as the words of the monument give it. It is known that the bodies of those who were killed at the Battle of Lexington were buried together at a spot on the northerly side of the Munroe plot or perhaps just outside it; there they rested till 1835, when the bodies were removed to the monument, then built, where they now remain.

I hesitate to record a criticism of Hudson's accuracy,— to call attention to his copy of the inscription on the monument. "Sacred to liberty and the rights of mankind" reads the strong, virile, noble epitaph of Parson Clarke. "Sacred to the liberty and the right of mankind" is the enfeebled copy as I find it on page 217 of the town history. The men of 1775 periled their lives in the sacred cause of Liberty in its absolute and concrete form. Note that Parson Clarke gives the word "liberty" first, making it superior to and inclusive of the rights of mankind and of the freedom and independence of America. The epitaph is a masterly and noble production and has often been referred to. Pity that the pith of its first and strongest line should have been taken out by the insertion of an offending article.

Joshua Simonds, who died in 1805 and is laid in the old burying-ground, was in the meeting-house with the town powder on the 19th of April when the British came up to the common. He was determined, if the enemy came into the church, to blow up the powder, even if his own life were lost by the means. On the passage of the troops he found a straggling British soldier, whom he forced to surrender. He took his gun and marched the man to Burlington. There he delivered the prisoner and his gun to Captain Parker, and it is *this* gun, given by Parker's descendants to the State, which is now in the Representatives' Hall at the State House.

Mr. E. M. Robbins's granduncle, Thomas Robbins, was carrying milk to Boston on the 19th of April; he was met and made a prisoner near Alewive Brook in West Cambridge (Menotomy), and was brought to Buckman's Tavern with David Harrington, another prisoner, where they were released. Mr. E. M. Robbins had this fact from the original folk.

Benjamin Wellington, coming down the "Back Road," now Pleasant Street, in the East Village, was made a prisoner by the British, but was afterwards released, and made his way over Mount Independence to the common, and engaged in the contests of the day.

This record is copied from the monument, erected by his descendants, at the junction of the present Massachusetts Avenue and Pleasant Street in the East Village :

> Near this spot
> at early dawn on the
> 19th of April, 1775,
> Benjamin Wellington,
> a minute-man,
> was surprised by British
> scouts and dismissed.
> With undaunted courage
> he borrowed another gun and
> hastened to join his comrades
> on Lexington Green.
> He also served his country
> at White Plains and
> Saratoga.
> The first armed man
> taken in the Revolution.

A British soldier was buried in the ground of the Munroe purchase. He was wounded on the 19th of April, and carried to the Buckman Tavern, where he died on the 22d. He was buried at a spot near the Eustis monument. Mr. Eli M. Robbins had the exact spot pointed out to him by Abijah Harrington, who died within a few years. Harrington's father was sexton in 1775, had buried the soldier and knew the spot well. The exact spot has been pointed out to the writer. The grave should have a permanent mark.

The pathetico-tragic stone near the entrance of the burying-ground chronicles the fact that six out of seven children of the Child family died at tender ages, within eleven days of each other. It points, very likely, to diphtheria, or "throat distemper," as the nomenclature of that day gave it. Another case of five in one family, and still another of three, are of similar import.

The various forms of belief of our ancestors in the final resurrection seem to be brought out in the epitaphs in the Lexington and other burying-grounds. Without entering into a theological discussion, — the creed of our early New England people seems to have been thus summarized: Granted that there is a God, and that a future world will exist, the theology of some two hundred years ago seems to have provided that, at some indefinite future period — it may be centuries or æons hence — a phenomenon will occur which will be known as the Resurrection, when the actual graves will be opened, the constituents of our earthly, material bodies be drawn from the soil or marshaled from the air, with which they shall have incorporated themselves, and shall appear in earthly, not spiritual forms, before a tribunal which shall doom them, on a very indefinite form of decision, either to a fixed condition of perfect happiness, whatever that may imply, or by an equally uncertain line of demarcation to a certain condition of torture, physical or mental, through endless ages; this as the result of the few years of our earthly existence. To us of this material and free-thinking age, many questions arise and jostle together in our minds, seeking a solution; but let them pass. The question naturally comes up to us, with the reasoning powers which God has given us, if such arbitrary decisions of utter happiness or inevitable and unceasing torment are conformable to the love, the justice of the Supreme Being who rules our destinies. But that these views of the resurrection obtained in the years of long ago may be learned from some of the epitaphs.

Mary Buckman, wife of John Buckman, the senior, is made to say:

> Dear friends, for me pray do not weep;
> I am not dead, but here do sleep
> Within this solid lump of clay
> Until the Resurrection day;
> And here indeed I must remain
> Till Christ shall raise me up again.

And of Mary Chandler, daughter of Major John, who died so late as 1818, it was said:

> Like roses cropt in their bloom,
> She's carried to the silent tomb,
> There speechless in dust to lie
> Till the trump sounds on high.

It is an interesting point, though it may be thought a minor one, to consider the character of the stones used for memorials. In the impecunious condition of our early ancestors, it is undoubtedly the fact that *no* stones, or else rude pasture stones, were used to mark the final resting-place. As a warmer regard for the decedents dawned on the survivors, or, perhaps, more money was obtainable, a certain sacredness attached to the place of sepulture, and more elaborate forms of stone, or at least some stones, marked the place of burial.

The cast-off body was committed to the earth, but the sentiment of those who were left behind showed itself by a species of evolution in the general tenor of the epitaphs. The bald theology of the earlier years became softened by the milder tenets of more recent belief. The dictum of the

early pastor that children dying in infancy were doomed to
everlasting perdition ; that the cry of the sorrowing mother,
authentically reported, was answered by the stern New England minister that there was no hope for the child who had
died, and that hell was paved with infant skulls — such
belief, or, at least, forms of words simulating belief, has
passed away, and the faith of modern Christianity regarding the "little children" has come back to the words of
the Saviour, — "of such is the kingdom of heaven."

How touching is the epitaph of Henry True Brown :

> This lovely bud, so young and fair,
> Called hence by early doom :
> Just come to show how sweet a flower
> In Paradise would bloom.

The epitaph was originally written in 1819 by Leigh
Richmond, and may be found over the grave of Ann
Steatt at Islington, near London.

A few more quaint epitaphs may be noted.

Of Mrs. Sarah Childs it is said :

> Friends nor physicians could not save
> My mortal body from the grave :
> Nor can the grave confine me here
> When Jesus calls me to appear.

David Cutler :

> No house of pleasure 'bove ground
> Do I expect to have,
> My bed of rest for sleeping found
> I've made the silent grave.

Mrs. Sarah Dudley :

> Christ my redeemer lives
> And often from the skies
> Looks down and watches all my dust
> Till he shall bid it rise.

Joseph Brown :

" who having for many years used the office of deacon well in the church of Christ in Lexington, purchased to himself a good degree and great boldness in the faith which is in Christ, who departed this life in the 86th year of his age."

There are many examples of the old epitaph :

> Behold, all you that passeth by,
> As you are now so once was I,
> As I am now so you will be,
> Prepare for death and follow me.

Indeed, this old verse has been much used in all burying-grounds from the time when it was rendered, in very old French, on the tomb of Edward, the Black Prince, in 1376, as it may be seen in Canterbury Cathedral, and as Pettigrew, in his collection of epitaphs, gives it in a dozen places in England.

Somewhat differently rendered we find it at Tichfield, in England, over the grave of James Steward in 1794, and repeated at Lexington :

> Time was I stood where thou dost now
> And view'd the dead as thou dost me :
> Ere long thou'lt lie as low as I
> And others stand and look on thee.

Of my ancestor, Ruhamah (Wellington) Brown, it is said:

> 'Tis but a few whose days amount
> To threescore years and ten:
> And all beyond that short account
> To sorrow, toil and pain.

It is a more cheerful anticipation which is figured in the epitaph of Mrs. Dorothy Tidd:

> While she sleeps beneath the sod
> We hope she's gone to rest with God.

It is a bit of stern realism which crops out in the epitaph which claims:

> Lo! in the law Jehovah dwells,
> But Jesus is concealed;
> Whereas the Gospel's nothing else
> But Jesus Christ revealed.

This is in a hopeful vein:

> No death is sudden to a soul prepar'd
> When God's own hour brings God's reward:
> Her death (and such, Oh reader, wish thy own)
> Was free from terrors and without a groan:
> Her spirit to himself the Almighty drew,
> Mild as the sun exhales the ascending dew.

It is a queer return to life to credit Abigail Seed, as shown by her epitaph, with the fact that she had

> "extra fingers and toes."

Was there, or not, a double meaning in the inscription at old Grey Friars in Edinburg, Scotland?

> Here snug in grave my wife doth lie;
> Now she's at rest, and so am I.

To speak once more of the character of the earlier gravestones, we find the evidence of native slate and native carving. When we come down nearer to our own time the slates are often of a different character, finer in texture, more carefully tooled, and with the inscriptions only put in by native workmen. In fact, this is the case all through the last centuries, — the seventeenth and eighteenth ; we are told that most of the gravestones were imported from Wales or England, quarried and carved in those countries, brought here as ballast and cut, so far as the inscriptions go, in this country. A glance at the gravestones in the Lexington burying-ground will show if this point be well taken.

Our ancestors were said to have had large families — and a study of the history of the town bears out this statement. It is, however, interesting to note that the rate of infant mortality was larger than obtains to-day, and that both adults and children succumbed to acute diseases which we to-day consider preventable and curable. With our modern knowledge of bacteria, of antisepsis and asepsis, and of regimen and nutritious food, we can easily see how great is their influence on the treatment of disease and its consequent mortality.

I may be pardoned for mentioning the markers of the Sons of the American Revolution, which have been placed by that society, in loving memory of those who periled their lives for the establishment of a separate, free and untrameled entity of our American people. The society, of which I have the honor to be president, cordially recognizes the indebtedness which they owe to the early inhabitants of Lexington, who on their own village green met, resisted and practically vanquished the soldiers of King George.

The epitaphs referred to in this paper will be published by the Lexington Historical Society in a separate volume.

THE CONCORD TURNPIKE.

READ BY A. BRADFORD SMITH, FEBRUARY 10, 1903.

Near the close of the eighteenth century and the beginning of the nineteenth, there were not many roads, and most of them were crooked and in bad condition. Until 1786 it was fourteen or fifteen miles from Lexington to Boston, going by the way of Harvard Square, thence through Brookline and Roxbury, over the neck to Boston. At one time there was a tablet in the square, with this inscription: "Seven miles to Boston," over the great bridge between Cambridge and Brighton. This bridge was built by Cambridge when Lexington was a part of it. The neck between Boston and Roxbury was one mile and 117 feet in length, and was the only way to Boston by land. The Charles River bridge connecting Boston to Charlestown was incorporated March 9, 1785, and was opened to public travel on the 17th of June, 1786; the bridge is 1,503 feet in length, 42 feet in breadth, and cost $50,000. The architect was Capt. John Stone. He was buried in Concord, and the following inscription is on his gravestone: "In memory of Capt. John Stone, the architect of that modern and justly celebrated piece of architecture, Charles River bridge. He was a man of good natural abilities, which seemed to be adorned with moral virtues and Christian graces. He departed this life in 1791, in the sixty-third year of his age."

There were not many modes of conveyance and but few carriages; farmers had to go to market with their horse and ox carts. The first improvement in transportation was the old Middlesex Canal, incorporated in 1789 and completed in 1808, at an expense of $828,000. That was an immense sum for those times. Its breadth at the surface was thirty feet; at the bottom, twenty feet, and the depth was four feet. This and other short canals on the Merrimac opened navigable communication between Boston and Concord, N. H., boats drawn by horses being used. They went at the great speed of three miles per hour. This was the first enterprise of the kind attempted in the United States. People from Lowell who wanted to go to Boston shopping would have to stay over night, as the trip took nine hours and the day was well spent when they arrived. This canal was in operation until the opening of the Boston & Lowell Railroad in 1835. After that the canal was used for the transportation of freight until somewhere in the forties. Another improvement was the building of the Newburyport turnpike, which was finished in 1806, at an expense of $420,000. Next followed the Lowell turnpike, built about 1806, the tollgate for which was near the residence of the late Charles Winship.

The third turnpike, upon which I base my paper, is the old Cambridge and Concord turnpike, running through the south part of Lexington.

An act to establish a corporation by the name of The Cambridge and Concord Turnpike Association.

Whereas, the highway leading from Cambridge through Lexington to Concord is circuitous, and the expense of making, straightening and keeping the same in good repair is much greater than can be reasonably required of said towns :

Section 1. Be it enacted by the Senate and House of Representatives in General Court assembled, and by the authority of the same, that Jeduthan Wellington, John Richardson, Thomas Heald, Francis Jarvis, Charles Wheeler, William Wheeler, Jonas Lee, Richard Richardson, John Stearns, Benjamin Kendall, Thomas Clarke, Peter Clarke, Ephraim Flint, Ephraim Flint, Jun., Daniel Brooks, Leonard Hoar, and Abiel Abbot, together with such others as may hereafter associate with them and their successors, be, and they hereby are made a corporation by the name and style of The Cambridge and Concord Turnpike Corporation, and by that name may sue and prosecute and be sued and prosecuted unto final judgment and execution; and shall have a common seal and exercise and enjoy all powers and privileges which are usually given and incident to similar corporations for making turnpike roads.

Beginning at or near the dwelling-house of Jonas Wyeth in Cambridge, near the common, and from thence to continue a westerly course, south of Dr. Andrew Craige's summer house" [near where the Cambridge Observatory now stands], "and on said course to the bridge, over the river out of Fresh Pond, so called" [now known as Alewive Brook]; "thence on said route about thirty feet south of the dwelling-house of Richard Richardson: thence on said route south of the dwelling-house of Joshua Kendall, in said Cambridge" [now Belmont]; "thence on the said course, near the dwelling-house of Joseph Underwood" [which is the first house west of Franklin Schoolhouse]; "thence on the said course near the dwelling-house of Benjamin Phinney" [better known as the Webster Smith place]; "then on said course by the dwelling-house of Thomas Tufts of Lexington; thence on said course near the dwelling-houses of Abiel Abbot, Leonard Hoar, Timothy Brooks and Daniel Brooks, in the town of Lincoln; thence on said course near the dwelling-house of Thaddeus Hunt in the town of Concord; thence on said course on as straight a line as circumstances will admit, to the meeting-house in Concord. And the said road shall not be less than four rods wide, and the path to be traveled in, not less than twenty-two feet wide in any part thereof; and when the said turnpike road shall be sufficiently made, and approved of by a committee appointed by the Court of General Sessions of the Peace, for the county of Middlesex, then the said corporation shall be authorized to erect two turnpike gates on the said road. And be it further enacted, that it shall be lawful for said corporation to demand and receive of each traveler or passenger, at each of the said gates, the following rates of toll, viz.: For every coach, chariot, phæton, or other four-wheel carriages drawn by two horses, twenty-five cents, and if drawn by more than two horses, an additional sum of four cents for each horse; for every cart or wagon drawn by two oxen or horses, ten cents, and if drawn by more than two oxen or horses, an additional sum of three cents for each ox or horse; for every curricle, fifteen cents; for every chaise, chair, or other carriage drawn by one horse, ten cents; for every man and horse, five cents; for every sled or sleigh drawn by two oxen or horses, an additional sum of two cents, for each ox or horse; for every sled or sleigh drawn by one horse, five cents; for all horses, mules, oxen or neat cattle, led or driven, besides those in teams and carriages, one cent each; and for all sheep and swine, at the rate of three cents by the dozen, and in that proportion for a greater or less number. And the said corporation shall at each place where the said toll shall be collected, erect and keep constantly exposed to open view, a sign or board, with the rates of toll of all the tollable articles, fairly and legibly written thereon, in large or capital characters. And be it further enacted, that if any person shall willfully or maliciously cut, break down or otherwise injure or destroy either of the said turnpike gates or signboards, or shall dig up or carry away any earth from the said road, or in any manner damage the same, or shall forcibly pass or attempt to pass the said gates by force without having first paid the legal toll at such gate, such person shall forfeit and pay a fine not exceeding forty dollars, nor less than two dollars, to be recovered by the treasurer of the said corporation. And be it further enacted, that the first meeting of the said corporation shall be held at the house of Phinehas Paine, inn-holder in Concord, on the fourth Tuesday in March inst., at two of the clock in the afternoon, for the purpose of choosing officers, who shall be sworn to the faithful discharge of his trust. And each proprietor in the said turnpike road, or by his agent duly authorized in writing, shall have a right to vote in all meetings of the said corporation, and shall be entitled to as many votes as the said proprietor has shares in the same; provided his number of said shares do not exceed ten; but no proprietor shall be entitled to more than ten votes, for any greater number of shares he may possess. And be it further enacted, that the said corporation shall be liable to pay all damages which shall happen to any person from whom toll is demandable by this act, for any damage which shall arise from any defect of bridges, or want of repairs within the same way; and shall also be liable to a fine, on the presentment of the Grand Jury, for not keeping the same way or the bridges thereon in good repair.

In the House of Representatives, March 7, 1803, this bill having had three several readings, passed to be enacted.

JOHN C. JONES, Speaker.

In Senate, March 7, 1803. This bill having had two several readings, passed to be enacted.
DAVID COBB, President.

March 8, 1803. By the Governor approved.
CALEB STRONG.

A true copy. Attest:
JOHN AVERY, Secretary.

After the road was completed the directors proceeded to erect two tollgates, and one was built near the residence of the late Leonard Hoar of Lincoln, the other about one-half mile west of Fresh Pond, near the estate of Richard Richardson, who afterwards opened a hotel. Then Mr. Leonard Hoar concluded to open a public house near the junction of Concord Avenue and the road leading to Lincoln Center. After the completion of the turnpike, a worthy minister from Concord drove over the road in his chaise one Sunday morning. A few moments afterward a part of the road over which he had driven disappeared from sight. There was an advertisement in the Boston papers, which read as follows: "Lost — A part of the Cambridge and Concord turnpike. Whoever will return the same will be suitably rewarded." A part of the road which disappeared was over a piece of meadow and the weight of the gravel caused the overflow.

When this turnpike was built, it was customary to go in a straight line, and this road went over nearly all the hills between the two places, which might have been avoided and the distance increased comparatively little, and then it would have been one of the most attractive thoroughfares in the county. A line of stages ran over this road, but owing to the hills and bad condition of the road, they were soon discontinued. It is my impression that Jeduthan Wellington was the first president of the corporation, and his house was located a few rods northeast of the Belmont town hall. He was nicknamed Jed Wellington; and the large hill in Belmont went by the name of "Jed's Hill" for many years. The road did not prove a very paying investment, and, after several assessments on the stockholders, they petitioned the county commissioners to lay it out as a county road in 1828. After it became a county road, the abuttors, when they reset their fences or walls, brought them into the road from one to ten feet. I know one man who brought his fence in ten feet, and there are places on the road not much more than fifty feet between the walls. About thirty or forty years ago Lincoln people altered the grade of the hills in that town, which greatly improved the road.

The section of the town near the turnpike was very dear to the gifted Theodore Parker, who was born in close proximity to it, and traveled over the road to school. As he was a lover of nature, all the birds and trees in that vicinity were dear friends, and he analyzed their special gifts and protected them from harm. There was a very tall pine-tree on the turnpike that was a landmark for miles around. It was said Mr. Parker, hearing that it was to be cut down, went to the owner, saying that if he would spare that tree he would pay him what he would receive for the wood. Suffice it to say the tree remained, the owner being too kind-hearted a man to take the proffered bounty. Recently, when a fire swept through those woods, the tree was so badly affected that its life-sustaining power was gone, and it was deemed advisable to cut it down. It was known for some time as the "Parker Pine," and the present owner of the estate thinks of erecting a summer house on the old site.

Many pleasant recollections cluster round the Concord

turnpike, which come forcibly to mind as I recall the past, — tender remembrance of large and worthy families who dwelt on this road and tilled the soil or were diligent in other vocations, most of them now scattered, and many of them reaping the reward of work well done, in the heavenly home. The road still remains one of the loveliest and most retired in our town, richly beautiful in natural scenery, abounding in fine, noble trees and lovely wild-flowers ; much used for pleasure driving in the summer and fall. As the old turnpike is quite a factor in the past of our town, may coming generations cherish this road, rich now with so much beauty!

EARLY DAYS OF THE LEXINGTON HIGH SCHOOL.

READ BY MISS MARY E. HUDSON, OCTOBER 13, 1903.

With the close of the present school year, the Lexington High School completes the first half-century of its history, and, to some of us who saw its small beginnings, it has seemed a fitting thing that some record should be made of the vicissitudes which marked its early career, while it was fighting its hard fight for continued existence.

In the year 1716, as the town records show, the first public school of Lexington was established on Lexington Common. One hundred and thirty-eight years of slow development were required before the citizens of Lexington, in town meeting assembled, in May, 1854, made the first appropriation for a high school in the town. A primary and grammar school in each of the two villages and an ungraded school in three outlying districts made up the educational system of Lexington at that time, and, in this, the town was in no way behind her sister towns of the same population and money valuation. Private schools of varying degrees of excellence had from time to time been established in our midst and, one after another, had closed a precarious existence with few to mourn their untimely end. To country academies or young ladies' seminaries went a few of our more favored youth, but for the most of our young people the district school was the only alma mater. But a new day was dawning in the educational world. High schools were springing up on every side and the day of the village academy seemed drawing to a close. In 1853 the question of a high school for Lexington was first publicly discussed, but failed to gain popular support. In the following year, 1854, a vigorous movement was made, a committee was appointed to consider the subject in all its lights, and, at an adjourned town meeting in May, the committee reported unanimously in favor of the project and recommended an appropriation of five hundred dollars "for high-school purposes," the regular school appropriation at that time, being twenty-five hundred.

The report was vigorously assailed. Conservatives, in bursts of dramatic oratory doubted the wisdom of the new departure; but the broader spirit of our citizens triumphed over all opposition, the munificent appropriation was made, and the Lexington High School was an established institution in the town.

To the school committee was assigned the duty of providing a suitable room for our reception, and the upper chamber in the town hall was selected for the purpose. Here on the morning of September 4, 1854, with hearts beating high with eager anticipations, we gathered, twenty girls and ten boys, the first pupils in the first term of the new high school.

With curious eyes, as we climbed the winding stairs, we inspected our new surroundings, and, when compared with the attractive classrooms our successors enjoy to-day, it cannot be said our quarters were palatial. This upper room in the town hall, intended for occasional use as a committee room, was but poorly adapted to the needs of thirty well grown pupils, and to those who have known that room only as a recitation room or chemical laboratory, it may well be an enigma how we adapted ourselves to such restricted quarters. The chamber was just thirty feet long and twenty-two feet wide. Lighted only from one end, blackboards around three sides darkened it still more. The three uncurtained windows were not over clean and the arched ceiling was none too white. At the left of the entrance door, on a slightly raised platform, stood the teacher's table. Facing that door and table were three rows of double desks exactly accomodating the thirty pupils who presented themselves for admission. These desks, with the necessary recitation seats, so filled our limited quarters that one can readily understand how the gymnastic exercises enjoyed by the pupils of a later day would have been quite impossible for us. Indeed, I remember how, when our first teacher indulged in some of his peripatetic wanderings up and down our narrow aisles, he sometimes came in sudden and unpleasant collision with the sharp corners of our desks.

At the right of the entrance door there stood a big, black, clumsy stove, a hungry devourer of coal, from which the resulting amount of heat was lamentably small. Up from this monstrous structure there rose, with numerous elbows, an ugly smokepipe which meandered along the ceiling until it disappeared in a hole in the opposite wall. No doubt a chimney was somewhere there concealed, but it has left no impress on my memory.

On the rear wall of the room, above the central window, there appeared a strange, box-like excrescence of unpainted pine, popularly termed a ventilator. The opening and shutting of a valve in its front regulated, theoretically, the ventilation of the room; but, as the ventilator never was finished and the connection with the outside air never established, it made little difference to us when the string attached to the valve broke off and the structure ceased a pretence of usefulness. With a heated stovepipe over our heads, no oxygen to speak of to supply thirty pairs of vigorous lungs, and no outlet for the vitiated air but a small open funnel hole over the teacher's desk, leading into one of the anterooms facing the street, well was it for our peace of mind that we knew nothing of germs and microbes in those days, and plodded on in happy ignorance of the direful perils we were incurring day by day.

Here in this room the high school began its work, and while the season continued mild we were well content with our surroundings. But there came a day, and all too soon it came, when bodily discomfort gravely interfered with mental growth and development. The winter of 1854 and 1855 was a hard one, and our schoolroom was very cold. The floor, through whose yawning seams the cold wind came in gusts, was like ice to our aching feet, and many were the expedients by which we strove to better our condition. Pieces of carpeting, thick shawls and hot soapstones were placed under our feet, and one enterprising girl carried a big, big squirrel muff, in whose recesses she buried her hands during the walk to school, and her feet when the school was reached. We tested the temperature one bitter day by placing on the floor, near the window, a tin cup half filled with water, and watched with curious eyes the ice formation which followed very soon. One young girl, whose abundant tresses lent themselves readily to the then favorite fashion of flowing curls, came to school one morning with her falling locks still damp from the hand of the hairdresser. The way was long and the mercury down in the zeros, and before her destination was reached those curling locks were stiff. Tradition says that all through that long, cold day in that arctic schoolroom those frozen ringlets never thawed out. I do not vouch for this, but I give it on the authority of a lady who is now a grandmother and whose reputation for truth and veracity has ever been above suspicion.

This state of things could not long continue without a vigorous protest from the sufferers, and our grievances were laid before the school committee with all due force and directness. Truth compels the admission that the reception we met was almost as cold as our schoolroom. Theoretically, that big stove was sufficient for all our needs. If fact and theory disagreed the committee argued that the fault was ours, and one bitter morning a reverend member of the Board made his appearance in our midst with the avowed purpose of proving to us by practical demonstration that dire ignorance in managing our fire was the cause of all our distress. The boy pupil who usually acted as fireman was excused from duty for the time, and with a confidence in his own success which was beautiful to behold, our good friend Mr. Leland took his place. All through that long forenoon he poked and he shoveled, he watched the thermometer and he rattled the grate till he grew red in the face and warm from exercise, though all else in the room was cold.

We gave our studies but a divided attention that morning as with curious eyes we watched his countenance, from which the look of triumph was fast fading away as the stubborn mercury refused to climb above its accustomed level. When the mid-day intermission came, with a grace which won our respect and admiration, Mr. Leland acknowledged his defeat and promised us immediate relief, if relief were possible. Accordingly a second stove was introduced into the corner diagonally opposite the first,— a small cylindrical affair, as modest and unpretending as the other was big and impudent. The only apparent result was that two or three seats in its immediate vicinity were made unpleasantly warm, another heated funnel was over our heads and the rest of the room was just as cold as ever.

Recognizing the hopelessness of the situation, we accepted the inevitable with what grace we might, helped, it may be, by the fact that our own homes, in 1854, were not the hothouses some of us know to-day. Furnaces were by no means the rule, the steam radiator was seldom seen, and hot-water heat was quite unknown.

Our familiarity with cold halls and draughty corners may have helped us bear the discomforts of our schoolroom. Be that as it may, we shivered through the winter and escaped from its rigors with no serious injury to health or happiness.

Our first teacher, Mr. George Washington Dow, was a graduate of Waterville, Me., and came to us, I think, from a school in Providence. It cannot be claimed for him that, either in personal characteristics or in literary attainments, he was an ideal instructor for the young. In early life he had been a common sailor on board a whaling ship and many were the reminiscences of wintry seas and arctic ice with which he regaled his youthful pupils. That he worked his way out of such environments and, turning his back on whaleboat and harpoon, sought and won a degree from one of our rural colleges, would certainly indicate a steadiness of purpose and an aspiration for something better than his early manhood promised. When he came to Lexington his youth was already past, he had little polish of manner or grace of speech, and in many ways he fell short of what we now consider essential in a high-school principal. But we must never forget that the standards of those days were not the standards of to-day. The modest stipend he received could hardly have attracted a teacher of a higher grade, while the uncertain future which faced this new high school during this, its trial year, made it impossible to procure what, even in that day, the committee might have desired. So, under all the circumstances, they undoubtedly did their best. Under these conditions, and hampered by these restrictions, our high-school days began, and to Mr. Dow's resolute purpose and his enthusiasm for his work we undoubtedly owed much of the success which marked our opening year.

Opposed by some of our leading citizens, we knew our school was on trial for its life, and for six long hours each day teacher and pupils, with what strength they might, worked for the cause which affected them all so nearly. There was little of system in our course of study. We entered when we pleased and withdrew when convenience or inclination dictated. Under these circumstances, the grade of the school could not be high. In some things it may have fallen below the standard of a well-ordered grammar school of the present day; but it was a decided advance on what we had ever known before, and with an honest pride we strove to maintain the advantage thus far gained.

Latin, French, history, rhetoric and a little of the natural sciences held a place in our curriculum, but in mathematics in its various forms and in a thorough knowledge of our mother-tongue lay our strength, our pride and our ambition. We studied plain old English grammar, and we plodded through Greene's Analysis till we knew every subject and predicate in the language and were as familiar with compound subjects and predicates as with the simplest words of our vocabulary. The many details may have faded from our memories, but I think the underlying principles remain. Half a century ago the spelling-book still held an honored place in every well-ordered schoolroom, and pleasant memories still linger of the old-fashioned spelling-matches with which we occasionally varied the monotony of our daily written exercises. Well would it be for some of us to-day, if we yet retained the skill we then acquired.

In foreign tongues our principal could not be called a proficient, but he drilled us in the intricacies of the French Grammar as resolutely as he schooled us in our own, and on the Latin declensions and conjugations we practised till they reeled off our tongues with the regularity of clockwork. The Roman pronunciation had not then obtained in school or university, and we rendered the Latin words in the good, old-fashioned English way.

Although his accent may not have been Parisian, nor his translations remarkable for elegance of diction, Mr. Dow's mathematical proficiency atoned for many defects. In the long hours on the whaleship, in the silence of the arctic seas, he had studied into the intricacies of navigation, and the results served him well in the work of his later life. We were drilled in arithmetic, algebra and geometry with a thoroughness not soon to be forgotten nor lightly to be valued. Good old Colburn's Mental Arithmetic had not then quite passed into disuse, but he substituted for it improvised mental exercises of his own dictation which answered every purpose and possessed the added merit of unexpectedness. Few of his pupils will soon forget the mental computations which formed a regular part of our weekly work. At his dictation we added six, multiplied by eight, subtracted seventeen and divided by nine, until a woman's most difficult task, the reckoning of her change on a shopping expedition, lost half its terrors in the years that were to come. Not all of us were experts in this mental work. We soon learned who would solve the problem first, and I may here be allowed to say that the hand which was often the first to wave triumphantly in air was the hand which, in·later years, guided up the hill of knowledge so many of our younger boys and girls. If the tree be known by its fruit, then that successful private school which so long occupied

Cary Hall should speak something in behalf of the Lexington High School in this, its opening year.

As a relief from the monotonous round of our daily tasks, our Fridays were made memorable by the literary exercises of our afternoon sessions. Selected readings, declamations and original compositions made up a programme of unquestioned interest to our auditors, whatever may have been the sentiments of the trembling participants.

The stammering speech of a frightened schoolboy must have done scant justice to the ponderous words of Webster or Calhoun, and the musical flow of Mrs. Hemans' lines found a poor interpretation in the half-audible rendering of a bashful girl. But greater the trepidation and far more painful the nervous strain when, one by one, in obedience to a merciless school law, we rose in our places to read, for the benefit of our visiting relatives and friends, the poor, crude productions of our untried pens. Under more favorable conditions, with a competent instructor to teach us elocution and to curb our rhetorical flights, these exercises might have been of lasting benefit to us all. But, alas, no such conditions existed. The girls, with some honorable exceptions, inclined to a high-flown, sentimental style of composition, tinged, for some unexplained reason, with a hopeless melancholy, quite at variance with the bright, happy spirit of the writers.

No topics were assigned us by our teacher, but, in the selection of our themes, the world was all before us where to choose. We seem to have developed a striking taste for fiction, and our youthful imaginations conjured up such tales of misfortune, sorrow and death as might well have hopelessly depressed any other than the happy, light-hearted girls we really were. The cardinal virtues, the weightiest questions in ethics, we sometimes discussed with a confidence in our own youthful judgments which proved anew how readily " fools rush in where angels fear to tread."

If in an ungarded moment our natural good spirits resumed their sway and, true to our own cheerful selves, we penned some bright, girlish lines, it was done in a half-apologetic way, and we soon fell back into a becoming sobriety of tone, and delighted our listening friends with such cheerful topics as " The Exile's Deathbed," " The Tolling Bell " and " The Cradle and the Grave," and all indited in such a high-flown redundancy of style as seems, to-day, more sad than the themes we chose.

A queer old gentleman said, one day, to a certain young lady who shall be nameless, " It seems to me you're pretty circumlocutory." No word that eccentric old man ever coined could better describe our literary style, and it needed the merciless criticism of a truthful, if less flattering, home auditory before some of us realized that plain, straightforward English was better than flowery rhetoric or too much circumlocution.

Sometimes we ventured into poetry, and here, indeed, we needed the wholesome discipline of the censor's pencil. There were rhymes that jingled, and there were lines that glowed with the true poetic fire amid much that was weak, frivolous and childish ; but the friendly critic was wanting and the real value of those literary afternoons may well be a question for future instructors to ponder.

But however sentimental or lachrymose might be the effusions of the young lady pupils, a sterner spirit pervaded what we called " the boys' side " of the room. Their themes took a loftier flight. The political skies of those days were dark and threatening. They were the days of Bleeding Kansas, of Border Ruffians, and of the murderous assault on Charles Sumner in the Senate of the United

States. The ear of the watchful listener already caught the mutterings of the coming storm. Our young high-school boys heard the sound and responded with bursts of florid patriotism. Very youthful their words were, no doubt, and, sometimes very diverting to their elders; but in the test which followed they all *rang true*, and when, in a few short years, the great crisis came and our country called on her loyal sons to rally to her defence, ten of our high-school boys responded to the call. It is with pride that we remember, to-day, that from out our ranks went Lexington's first volunteer, Edward F. Chandler.

In connection with our literary exercises we issued a weekly paper, "The Scholars' Offering" by name, on whose editorial staff we served in groups of four, our term of service extending over one issue of the paper. One young gentleman acted as editor-in-chief, with three young ladies as assistants in his work. It would be difficult to determine the exact head under which to class this ambitious sheet. It was in no way a newspaper. No suspicion of yellow journalism could ever attach to its pages. Perhaps the legend "Good, easy reading," which heads, to-day, a certain Boston daily, would best describe "The Scholars' Offering" in the first years of its existence. Typewriters were unknown in 1854, and in the miscroscopic handwriting peculiar to the period the editors transferred, to the monstrous sheet of blue foolscap, the editorials they penned and the contributions they begged from their kindly fellow-pupils. The heading of the sheet, a marvel of elaborate German text, was the work of a good-natured boy (Samuel E. Chandler) who loved his pencil better than he loved his Latin, and gave to many a scroll and flourish the energy which might better have been bestowed on geometrical problems or puzzling lines in Virgil. It was not many years before he wore the Union blue, and lay, a wounded prisoner, in the depths of Libby Prison. We have his own assurance that the memory of those happy, easy-going days in the old high-school brightened many a dark and weary hour of that seemingly hopeless captivity.

Shielded behind some fanciful nom-de-plume, in the columns of the Offering, we gave free rein to the exuberant spirits so rigidly curbed in our more ambitious productions. No joke was too silly, no riddle too absurd, no parody too atrocious, for our vandal pens. One ambitious young poetess, I remember, from an imaginary viewpoint at the beginning of the then distant Twentieth Century, pictured the Lexington High School as she fancied it might be at the very date at which we, in reality, are standing now. Was it a foreshadowing of the beautiful new building of to-day which inspired the lines,

"Where the schoolroom stood, stands a lofty dome,
'Neath whose roof, 'mid whose aisles, I often roam"

And did she foresee something of the ignominious fate of its humble predecessor when she closed with the remarkable statement,

" The horned cattle feed in the old schoolroom."

A proper sense of our dignified position as pioneers in the high-school ranks should, perhaps, have placed us above the need of any kind of discipline, but truth compels me to say that we were very human boys and girls, and sometimes sorely needed a master's restraining hand. We were disciplined, largely, by means of what we knew as a Deduction Paper, a big, blue sheet which adorned our teacher's desk, and on which our names were relentlessly inscribed. Did we laugh, did we whisper, did we stumble in a recitation, did we indulge in any of the many peccadillos so dear to the average scholar's heart, down went a black mark against our names. That awful mark was known as a deduction, though from what the deduction was made, or what was the system of ranking, if indeed we were ever ranked at all, I think only our teachers ever knew. We only knew that, in some remote way, it was a mark of disgrace, and that against some of us the list was ominously long.

But there were days, and stirring days they were, when no Deduction Paper could curb the turbulent spirit of those eager boys and girls. No one of us, I think, can soon forget that mild spring morning when rebellion swept like a cyclone through our ranks, bringing pupils and Committee in fierce collision and leaving wrath and destruction in its track. We went to our school, on the morning of May 1, 1855, a class of orderly, law-abiding pupils. In two short hours we stood, a band of angry insurgents, casting law and order to the winds, and bidding defiance to the vested authorities of the town. The causes of the conflict were too remote to be recounted here. I am not sure that we clearly remember them ourselves; but they spurred us on to such energetic action as astonished our opponents and surprised ourselves no less. We fully believed in the righteousness of our cause, but our belief might have been expressed in a less aggressive and more conciliatory manner. At the close of the action, victory perched on neither banner. Before the sun went down that night, our valiant teacher, in whose behalf we fought the battle, had made his individual peace with his offended superiors, generously laying on us who had been his ardent champions the entire blame for the encounter.

But, though the leader deserted, the rank and file stood firm. For one week the school was closed. For one week those youthful rebels, " pride in their port, defiance in their eye," stalked up and down our village street, saying, with John Parker, " If they want a war, let it begin here." At the week's end neither party capitulated, but the school reopened. We were summoned back to our abandoned tasks, and finished our school year without further incidents. It may be added, in passing, that our teacher, Mr. Dow, was finished also, and when the school year ended he folded his tent like the Arabs and as silently stole away.

Those naughty boys and girls are order-loving men and women now, not over-proud of the part they played on that eventful morning, but no history of that first year at the high-school would be complete with this, its most exciting episode, left out. The echoes of the conflict have long since died away, but through the silence of the many intervening years I hear, in fancy, the old childish rhyme, which best determines the relative merits of the contest,

> "You both were wrong,
> And both were right,
> And both were very impolite."

Perhaps it was well for the future of our school that the question of its continuance for another year had already been decided. The opposition was by no means dead, but the hard, honest work we did during that first trial year and the creditable showing made at our public examinations had changed into firm supporters many who had once been but lukewarm in our cause. At the annual town meeting in March, 1855, the citizens gave us their unqualified indorsement by doubling the high-school appropriation of the previous year, besides making a small addition to the amount raised for the several district schools in the town. There were anxious hearts awaiting the verdict that day, and when the glad news reached him, one enthusiastic boy, with a zeal far outrunning the limited means at his command, by a salute on Belfry Hill from one old musket, supplemented by a bunch of firecrackers, announced to a listening world that our cause was won, and the Lexington High School had taken on a new lease of life.

Transferred from our dimly lighted upper chamber to the larger, more airy and far more cheerful lower hall, under the direction of a teacher whose youthful energy and broader culture left their unquestioned impress on the pliant minds of his pupils, the high school, in September, 1855, entered on its second year of work and usefulness, — a work which has broadened far beyond the bounds our eyes could then discern and a usefulness whose limits we may not, even now, accurately measure.

With our standard of scholarship a little higher, our curriculum a little broader and our methods a little more in keeping with the recognized system of the day, we gave to our new principal, Mr. H. O. Whittemore, a more hearty co-operation than his predecessor could command, and a gradual gain in the standing of the school was the direct result. We still had obstacles to encounter. Cold as our upper room had been, the heating properties of the furnace in the lower hall were even more unsatisfactory, and during the three cold winter months we went back to our attic and tried to tell ourselves that we were comfortable. For the rest of the year the lower room was our home, and we dwelt there undisturbed, save when the approach of one of Lexington's numerous town meetings brought us an enforced vacation, while our desks were hurriedly taken up and huddled into a corner and the room was restored to its original status as a town hall. But, notwithstanding these minor drawbacks, it was a bright, sunny, happy period in the history of the high school, and marked a decided advance in the town's educational standing.

It is not the province of this paper to follow the later fortunes of the school. If in this imperfect sketch of its opening year I have given any adequate idea of the restrictions and obstacles we faced, and have shown, in ever so poor a way, the contrast between *then* and *now*, my purpose will be quite fulfilled.

Who were those first scholars in the Lexington High School, and how have they used the privileges they enjoyed? There were familiar Lexington names on that school register. There were Whitman and Bridge and Parker and Turner and Phelps and Butters and Knight and Nash and Pierce and Muzzey and Chandler and Saville and Goodwin and Bryant, and many more with which I will not weary you to-night. From all quarters of the town they came, and here, for the first time, East Lexington, Scotland, Kite End and Concord Hill met on common ground in the center of our good old Lexington. Together we worked with a will and an earnestness which cold and discomfort could not overcome, and into the work of life, which came to us so soon, we carried many a memory which is priceless to us to-day. There are gray heads among those scholars now. There are devoted mothers and grandmothers, there are veteran and honored teachers, there are upright and successful business men, among our numbers. Some have served their town in positions of trust and honor, some have bled for their country on Southern battlefields, and some are sleeping in soldiers' graves, to-day, over which the Grand Army flag floats in perpetual remembrance.

And we tenderly recall one bright, strong, merry-hearted girl, one of the bravest and noblest of us all, who, after years of successful work in the Boston schools, gave herself, heart and soul, to the study of a chosen profession, and fell by the wayside, just as she had gained, with marked distinction, the goal she so much coveted.*

When we remember these, there are, indeed,

> " things of which we may not speak,
> There are dreams that cannot die,
> There are thoughts that make the strong heart weak,
> And bring a pallor into the cheek
> And a mist before the eye."

Those pleasant high-school days are long since past. The places that once knew us know us no more. Our dear old building, shorn of its architectural beauty, has descended to a level too pitiful to contemplate. The hurrying steps of our successors have long since trodden out the last faint footprint we left behind; but, with hearts that still warm to the memories of the dear old days and beat with cordial sympathy for those who follow where we led the way, we, the pioneers of the Lexington High School, extend to the pupils of to-day our warm congratulations, simply reminding them that, unto whom so much more has been given, of them shall very much more be required.

---

* Dr. Martha F. Whitman

CLOCK-MAKING IN LEXINGTON.

READ BY MISS ELIZABETH W. HARRINGTON, FEBRUARY 10, 1903.

Very few facts relating to the manufacture of clocks in Lexington have been preserved. The first clocks were made by the Mullikens, and many are now in existence still keeping excellent time. Robert (or Benjamin) Mulliken came from Glasgow, Scotland, to Boston, Mass., an emigrant, in 1683, at the age of eighteen, and moved to Bradford, Mass., between the years 1683 and 1688. He was the first gravestone maker in Essex County, producing headstones between 1723 and 1737. While the gravestones seemed to mark the end of Time, the descendants of Robert were bent on marking the progress of time, as most of them took up the business of clock-making, some in Newburyport and some in Bradford and later in Concord and Lexington. Nathaniel Mulliken and his brother Samuel, sons of the emigrant, made tall clocks in Bradford and peddled them around the country, as was the custom of the day, taking orders, or leaving a clock at each house to be tried and proved, much as sewing machines are left at houses for trial at the present day. In pursuit of his calling, on one propitious day, Nathaniel visited Lexington and set up one of his timepieces in the house of Deacon John Stone, near Lincoln. In the words of Mr. Hudson, "It would seem that the family were well pleased with the beating of the clock, and the heart of the youngest daughter beat so in unison with that of the maker that she was willing to leave the timepiece in her father's house and place herself in a situation where she would know more of the clocks and their young maker." Nathaniel Mulliken and Lucy Stone were married in 1751 and it was probably about this time that they came to live in Lexington, he buying the house and shop standing where Mr. Norris has built his house on Massachusetts Avenue, nearly opposite the lower entrance to the cemetery, and there set up the clock-making business and carried it on for about sixteen years, till he died in 1767. He was also a blacksmith and was very proud of the andirons he made in his blacksmith's shop, near the house. Mr. Norris tells me that in digging for his foundation about 1890, he found bricks and other indications of the cellar wall of the Mulliken house and shop. Nathaniel, 2d, with his mother, after his father's death, followed the business about ten years, till by the wanton act of the British soldiery, on their return from Concord, on the 19th of April, his house and shop were burned and he died the next winter, aged twenty-four. His loss was £431.

This second Nathaniel must have been very ingenious, for it is a fact that he invented a musical clock, which, in deference to the strict prejudices of our Puritan fathers, played psalm tunes on Sundays and Moll Brooks (or Marlbrook, intended to ridicule the old Duke of Marlborough) and other lively tunes on week-days. The works of this clock were removed and afterward found in the knapsack of a wounded British soldier in Malden or Medford. He made the clock lately owned by Miss Sarah Chandler, a descendant, and now owned by Mrs. George H. Reed.

Nathaniel's brother Joseph, having learned the trade of his uncle in Bradford, made clocks in Concord later. His brother John learned cabinet-making in Concord and followed the British down from there on the 19th of April, till he reached the burning ruins of his mother's house and shop, and with tears in his eyes declared he could go no farther. He subsequently had a shop across the road, nearly opposite his brother Nathaniel's shop, where he made the tall cases of the clocks and all the coffins used in town ; and there are many pieces of furniture now in Lexington which figured in the wedding outfits of that period.

Some of the clock dials were imported ; but we have sufficient proof that the elder Nathaniel, at least, cut the dials himself. One of his descendants, who was born and lived on the site of John's shop, tells me she well remembers when a child playing with cogwheels and a brass dial. In digging about the place where the shop stood, the models for casting cogwheels and the crucibles for melting the brass have recently been found. A pattern on which was marked the different sizes of cogwheels which Nathaniel used has been in an attic within the remembrance of the descendant before mentioned, now living; and for further proof that the works were made by the Mullikens, a jeweler in Fall River has recently taken to pieces one of their clocks and finds the works were all made by hand. Those clocks, the dials of which are ornamented by moons and maps, were made later than the Mulliken clocks.

I have been told by a clock-maker in Boston, of many years' experience, that it was the custom in those early days to place the name of the owner of the clock on the dial as often as that of the maker, making it difficult to decide by whom the clock was made, and the date was rarely given. Many clocks first set running one hundred and fifty years ago are now in good condition. In the house of my great-grandfather, Daniel Harrington, then standing back of the common on what is now Elm Avenue, a Mulliken clock, made in 1772, ticked out the momentous hours on the morning of April 19, 1775, while my ancestors stood on the green facing the enemy. It has never been out of the family and is now in Wheeling, W. Va., in first-rate condition.

Could the old clocks speak in any but the language of Time, what interesting history they would unfold! Those of you who were fortunate enough to grow up in a home with one of them know how much it seemed like a living member of the family. Fashion set them one side, till the furore for all ancient furniture put a sudden value upon them. When they were made their price was about forty dollars; now the price often is above one hundred.

For the few facts I have been able to gather regarding the clock business in Lexington, I am indebted to Mr. Abbott Mulliken and to Mrs. Lydia Bacon, both living descendants of the clock-makers. The next I can learn of clock-making in Lexington is that in 1831 Chittendon and Burr started the business in the second story of the ell of the Jonathan Harrington revolutionary house, corner of Bedford Street and Elm Avenue, and carried on the business about five years. These clocks were all of wood, both works and cases, and were not tall clocks, but were hung on the wall. Mr. Chittendon bought the house of Mr. John Augustus, the philanthropist, who had used it for a shoeshop, but failed to succeed. This clock-making was very profitable, and the houses on the opposite side of Bedford Road, just above the old Normal School building (then the Academy), were used for business or for boarding the workmen employed. The firm afterward had a shop in the rear of the houses on Massachusetts Avenue, nearly opposite the railroad station. Miss Sarah Studley and Miss Louise Muzzey did most of the glueing and bronzing of these clocks, which were peddled along the road. Chittendon tried to buy land near the entrance of Bloomfield Street, not far from where the Mulliken clocks were made, but an agreement as to price could not be reached and he abandoned the project. Mr. Burr afterwards moved to Chicago. The business finally died out.

HOW THE HANCOCK-CLARKE HOUSE WAS SAVED.*

At the annual meeting of the Lexington Historical Society held Mar. 10, 1896, it was reported by a member that the old parsonage known as the Hancock-Clarke house was soon to be torn down, the proprietor having decided that it was no longer fit for occupancy and that she would make no repairs on it. After some discussion, a committee consisting of James P. Munroe, Hon. A. E. Scott, Rev. C. A. Staples, Mr. George O. Whiting and Mr. George O. Smith was appointed to see what could be done to prevent its demolition and save it for its historical associations and the honor of Lexington. On consultation with the owner, it was found impossible to save it on the spot where it stood, though a large sum was proposed for the house and a hundred feet square of ground whereon it stood. No money could buy it to have it remain there; it must be removed or destroyed; and it was learned that steps had already been taken to have it torn down. In this critical state of the matter, a member of the committee took the responsibility of buying the house and agreeing to move it off within sixty days, paying therefor the sum of $150. This action was reported to the Society at a special meeting held Oct. 24, 1896, and it was voted that the house should be retained on Hancock Street, that a subscription should be opened then

---

* This interesting account of the preservation of the Hancock-Clarke House gives no hint of the fact that its modest author, Rev. C. A. Staples, was the prime mover in the enterprise and has been the most active worker ever since. It was he who negotiated for the house and advanced the money for its purchase and removal; and through his influence a considerable part of the sum needed to save and restore the building was secured. — JAMES P. MUNROE.

and there for the purchase of a new site and the removal of the house, and that a committee of fifteen ladies be appointed to canvass the town for the raising of funds for these objects; and the following ladies were appointed, viz.: Mrs. J. H. Willard, Miss Miriam Garfield, Miss Emma O. Nichols, Mrs. Emma F. Goodwin, Mrs. H. A. C. Woodward, Mrs. Louise M. Peaslee, Mrs. Irving P. Fox, Mrs. James P. Munroe, Miss Elizabeth Harrington, Miss Rose B. Morse, Miss M. Alice Munroe, Miss Gertrude Pierce, Miss Alice M. Hunt, Miss Helen E. Griffiths, Mrs. F. C. Childs.

At this juncture, Mr. George Muzzey, owning the Kendall estate on the opposite side of the street, generously offered to divide it and sell seventy-five feet front for a new site, if the purchaser would grant the right of free entrance to the remainder. This was finally accepted by the purchaser of the old house, who paid $1,500 for the ground. Then followed the making of a new cellar and the removal to the new location, the reconstruction of the chimneys, re-shingling, painting and repairing of the venerable mansion, placing it in a fairly sound condition from cellar to garret. It was then turned over to the Society at the original cost of the house, ground, removal and repairs, which, including all expenses incurred, amounted to $3,107.42. In the mean time, the committee of ladies having in charge the collection of funds had faithfully performed their work, going from house to house throughout the town and receiving contributions from a few cents to a hundred dollars, from each person. Mrs. Edith C. Childs, acting as chairman of the committee, paid in the sum of $1,343, and other contributions from the town increased this amount to $1,545. Eleven patriotic societies of Massachusetts donated $1,040, and friends in other places, old residents of Lexington or their descendants, gave $740, of which one family, great-grandchildren of Rev. Jonas Clarke, gave $400, making a total altogether of $3,325 contributed to save this historic house, and leaving a balance of $221 in the treasury. This, with some additional funds, was used for furnishing the house. In raising the money for the first expenditure, two ladies contended for the honor of giving the original cost, — Miss Alice B. Cary, in memory of her mother who, forty years before, had wished to buy the place and present it to the town, offering to give $1,000 for that object ; and Mrs. C. M. Green of Boston, who claimed the honor as a great-granddaughter of Parson Clarke. She was permitted the pleasure and satisfaction of making the gift, and Miss Cary was allowed the privilege also of commemorating her mother's generous offer by a similar gift.

After the removal of the house and the completion of necessary repairs, on Oct. 12, 1897, the first regular meeting of the Society was held at the house; reports were made by various committees regarding the accomplishment of the work, and a general jubilation took place over the fact that this precious relic of the opening scenes of the great war for independence had been saved from destruction, and was the property of the Lexington Historical Society, free of all encumbrance. A committee was appointed consisting of Mr. Charles A. Wellington, Mrs. A. S. Parsons, Miss M. Alice Munroe, Rev. C. A. Staples and Mr. Charles B. Davis, to have charge of furnishing the house and of transferring the relics belonging to the Society from the Town Hall to this place. It was voted that the names of all persons who have contributed to the fund for the preservation of the Hancock-Clarke house, together with those of the committee that canvassed the town, be preserved in a permanent form in the house, a vote which has not been executed unto this day, but should be at once before more of the names are lost or forgotten. Many improvements have been made in the house since its occupancy by the Society, involving the expenditure of twelve or fifteen hundred dollars. These include the building of the small addition and the putting in of a large fireproof safe, concreting the cellar and placing iron posts under the house, electric lighting, a new furnace and provision for extinguishing fires, making altogether an expenditure for the entire property of $4,500, and putting it in safe and sound condition throughout, — a home of the Society of which we may well be proud.

The house was not provided with a regular attendant and caretaker until the summer of the following year, and the record of visitors, and contributions and sales, did not begin until June, 1898. Since then it has been kept continuously to the present time, and that we may see what the steady growth of interest on the part of the public has been in this historic house, I quote the following statistics from the record:

					Number of Visitors.	Contributions and Sales.
From June 1, 1898 to Dec. 31,				1899	4,829	$ 355
"	Jan. 1,	1900	"	"	1900	11,838	560
"	"	1901	"	"	1901	12,950	642
"	"	1902	"	"	1902	14,282	824
"	"	1903	"	"	1903	20,235	1,038
					64,134	$3,419

The Society is to be congratulated upon having rescued this priceless relic of two centuries ago from destruction, and upon receiving so emphatic an endorsement from the public of the wisdom of their action.

THE MUNROE TAVERN.

WRITTEN BY ALBERT W. BRYANT IN 1902 AND READ BY DR. F. S. PIPER, OCTOBER 11, 1904.

It would be difficult to select a place in Lexington embracing more notable events of the past than are connected with the historic " Munroe Tavern," surrounded as it is by many reminiscences, each one of sufficient merit to make a landmark of distinction. It is in this belief that I am influenced to record a few thoughts in relation to its past history, especially as it was the birthplace of Hiram Lodge, and its home for the first twenty-five years of its existence.

The Munroe Tavern property was a portion of what was called the " Pelham Farm," which was sold to John Poulter in 1693; it was the southeast corner of the Poulter land. In 1697, Ebenezer Nutting sells to Isaac Johnson twenty. acres of land, with a small dwelling-house and shop. In 1699, Isaac Johnson sells to John Comee land and a small dwelling on it; Comee married Martha Munroe, daughter of the first Munroe that settled in Lexington. In 1719, John and Martha Comee convey thirty acres of land to their son, David Comee, and the south end of the Merriam House, being all the old end, with the cellar, privilege of woodyard, and water from the well, and also land to build an addition to his father's barn. John Comee in a paper in the Essex Registry, describes himself as " inn keeper "; after he built the addition to the mansion house he probably kept a public house. In 1738, David Comee conveyed the buildings and twenty-six acres of land to John Overing of Lexington. In 1747, John Overing sold to John Buckman the Merriam House and twenty acres of land. John

Buckman died in 1763. His son John married, in 1768, Ruth Stone, daughter of Samuel Stone, who owned, at that time, what we call the Buckman Tavern (which is now the Stetson estate near the common).

John lived at what afterwards became the Munroe Tavern. He was a cabinet-maker, haberdasher, coffiner, cooper; he also had a potash house, and made potash on the premises in partnership with Edmund Munroe, who boarded with him after he married in 1768; they were in the potash business together and had a copper boiler. In 1770, John Buckman, cabinet-maker, conveyed to William Munroe, cooper, a mansion house, barn, workhouse, three-fourths of a potash house with works belonging to it, and twenty-six acres of land. Munroe had made improvements on the house at the time he purchased it. It was in 1770 that this property passed into the hands of William Munroe, and now belongs to his grandson.

When noting the characteristics of individuals of prominence, there is generally a desire to know something of their ancestry. As I intend to say a few words about Col. William Munroe, the first Master of Hiram Lodge, I will briefly allude to some of his progenitors. William Munroe, the ancestor of all the Munroes of Lexington, was born in Scotland in 1625 and came to this country in 1652. The first record of him is in 1657, when he was fined for not having rings in the noses of his swine. Tradition asserts that, taken as a prisoner of war in Scotland, he was sold to servitude to pay the expenses of his immigration, as was a custom in those times, and the claim was purchased by a Mr. Whittemore, or Winship, living near the line of what is now Lexington and Arlington. His term of service must have been short, for he was his own man in 1657.

He settled at Cambridge Farms about 1660, in the northeasterly part of the town, his house being near what is now the Woburn line, and several of his sons lived with him, or not far from him. It was said that his house resembled a rope walk, so many additions having been made to accommodate his sons as they settled in life, adopting a Scottish custom. He, in a measure, confined the Munroes together, giving the name to the locality which has ever been retained, — the "Scotland District."

Though he came to this country under unfavorable circumstances and set up for himself rather late in life, it appears that he was quite successful in worldly affairs, and had a large and prosperous family. He was interested in church and town affairs and contributed so liberally that his generosity was publicly acknowledged. He was a man of enterprise and character, which was made apparent by the offices of honor and responsibility conferred on him. He was forty years of age when he married, yet he reared a family of thirteen children. He was married three times, and had four children by his first wife, and nine by his second. He died in 1717, at the age of ninety-two. His inventory (against which there was no objection) at his death gave the following personal property to his wife: one bed and bolster ; one pillow ; one chest ; one warming-pan ; one pair of tongs, and one pewter platter.

William, son of the first William, was born in 1669, and was married twice, having seven children by his first wife and two by his second. He held many offices and was prominent in church and military affairs.

William, the third, was born in 1703, and died in 1747. He was on a committee to enlarge the burial ground, and was the first one buried in it. He left six children, the fourth child, William, the subject of this sketch, being born in 1742. He was married twice, and had six children by his first wife. He died in 1827.

My recollections of him extend from 1822 to 1827, the time of his death. It was my duty, when a lad, to drive my father's cows to pasture during the summer season, and in doing this I passed his house twice each day. It was his custom in pleasant weather to walk to the old tavern, then in charge of his son Jonas, his residence being about an eighth of a mile distant. The frequency of meeting him, and his appearance, enable me to recall to mind some of his peculiarities. He was short in stature, thick-set, broad-shouldered, with a very short neck. His steps were short and quick for a person of his age. He invariably wore a long-bodied coat and a broad-brimmed hat, with a staff in hand nearly as long as his height, with his hand placed about a third from the top. He was affable, social, with a disposition ever ready to enjoy a joke.

No citizens of Lexington have been more honored and respected than the Munroes; for their energy, their enterprise, and especially their interest in military affairs. They were quite prolific. The four families, of which an abstract is here given, had thirty-two children. About forty years since they began to disappear, so that at the present time there are only three families in town by that name, and these three families have but ten members.

Without the slightest desire of detracting from the bravery or patriotism of those Minute Men, who took part on the 19th of April, 1775, in resisting a foreign foe, unquestionably no one was more distinguished in rendering service than Col. William Munroe, the Orderly Sergeant of the Company of Minute Men. To substantiate this assertion, I herewith restate what has been often told of his judgment, as seen on the 18th and 19th of April, 1775, which is a correct representation of his character:

"When a man was returning from market, late in the

afternoon on the 18th of April, 1775, he called at the Munroe Tavern and informed Munroe that he had passed several British officers who were on their way to Lexington, and as the wind blew their overcoats open he saw that they were armed. Munroe, conceiving their purpose, or design, as quickly as possible gave the alarm (which was agreed upon) for the Minute Men to assemble on the Common. He selected eight men, armed, and placed them as guard around the house of Mr. Clark for the night, and remained with them. As the British officers had passed through town towards Concord, Munroe dispatched several men to follow them, to ascertain their whereabouts, and watch their movements. They were so unfortunate as to be captured when about midway between Concord and Lexington.

"It is reported that the evening of the 18th of April being chilly, those Minute Men who resided in the vicinity went home; others found accommodations at the Buckman Tavern. About midnight Revere appeared at Clark's house and requested an interview with Hancock and Adams; Munroe informed him that it was late when the family retired and they did not wish to be disturbed. Revere insisted, as his business with them was of that importance that it was imperative that he should at once see them, and he immediately rapped on the door. Mr. Clark hearing the rap at the door, raised a window and inquired what was desired. Revere informed him that he had some special information for Hancock and Adams. Hancock, hearing the conversation, and recognizing Revere's voice, said, 'Come in.'

"Munroe, upon hearing from Revere that the British troops were probably on their way to Lexington, sent at once a messenger towards Boston, who was to report as soon as possible. As time passed and the messenger did not return, the second one was sent. After waiting anxiously a reasonable time the third was sent on the same errand. The desire to know what had become of the three men was so intense that the fourth started on the same mission, which proved successful in solving the problem why the others did not return.

"As a precaution to conceal their movements, two soldiers were sent some distance in advance of the body of troops; these two soldiers would permit anyone to pass them, then capture such as passed, so that those sent to obtain information were easily taken. The horse of the fourth one seeing the two soldiers sitting beside the road, became frightened, and refused to proceed; while urging the horse, the rider caught a glimpse of the main body of troops, and at once started back, with all speed possible, to give the information anxiously desired.

"Munroe, upon receiving the fact of their approach, hastily summoned the company of Minute Men, and formed them in line, as they stood, when the British troops appeared before them."

It is evident that Munroe was engaged throughout the day, and it is presumed that after the skirmish in the morning he followed on towards Concord and, in the retreat in the afternoon, joined with others in the pursuit. Fortunate it was for him that he was not at home when the troops ransacked his house and killed John Raymond, who was in his employ, and had charge of the premises in his absence.

When Munroe came in possession of the tavern property in 1770, the additions which had previously been made gave the house probably the appearance it has at present. When the hall was added, the original looks were altered, and when the hall was subsequently removed, the house was restored to its former appearance.

There seems to be no definite knowledge whether the hall was built for the special use of Hiram Lodge or for general purposes. There is no exact date when it was added to the main building, but the supposition is that it was a short time previous to the institution of the lodge in 1797.

My recollection of it dates back to my boyhood days when, with other boys, it was used for our playground, and oftentimes some of the lodge implements were used in our boyish games. My familiarity with it continued by attending dancing-schools, dancing-parties, lectures and exhibitions, until it was removed about 1850.

The hall was sixty feet in length and twenty feet in width. On the east end the Master's chair was placed upon a platform six feet wide, raised eighteen inches above the floor, and reached by three steps. A board, of proper width for seating purposes, uncushioned, was permanently fastened to the east, west and north sides of the room, by wooden brackets. The entrance to the hall was about twenty feet from the east end, and on the south side of the room. A few feet from the entrance, towards the west, a large, open fireplace furnished heat. On the south side, near the west end, an alcove, or recess, about six feet wide, was reserved for storing settees, desks, and what was not needed for the purpose for which the hall was to be used. For lighting purposes tallow candles were used. They were placed beside each window, in what was called a "candle-holder." This was made from a strip of tin fifteen inches in length and four inches wide. About four inches of one end was bent at a right angle, with a socket to hold the candle upright. This was suspended by a nail driven in the window casement; a pair of candle snuffers perfected the lighting appliances. The carpet for the hall was the soft side of a pine board.

The hall was in common use for public purposes,— singing and dancing schools, lectures, exhibitions and social dancing-parties.

My earliest thought of any event connected with Freemasonary took place about eighty years ago, when a celebration on the 24th of June was held under the auspices of Hiram Lodge, having been at that time nearly, if not quite, twenty-five years in existence. The occasion must have been considered of more than ordinary importance, by the particular and elaborate arrangements that were made. I retain no remembrance of the exercises on that day, except the preparation for the dinner. A canvas tent, a hundred feet or more in length, and of sufficient width for three tables that would accommodate two hundred or more persons, for whom provisions were prepared, was erected in the rear of the house.

Jonas Munroe, who was known as "Uncle Jonas," was the landlord at that time; his success in providing for the banquet surpassed that which had hitherto been attempted. The reason that I have so clear a recollection of this part of the celebration, is, at that time it was customary to place the food upon the table before the company were seated; afterwards each one helping himself as he chose. Several young lads, including myself, watched with much earnestness the placing of the food upon the tables, and speculated if we should be lucky enough to get a piece of pie, a slice of plum pudding, or a wing or leg from one of those chickens. But the old maxim that there is many "a slip between the cup and the lip" was here fully verified. As the company were on the point of being seated at the tables a terrific shower of rain and wind suddenly burst forth, and with such violence that all upon the tables was either swept to the ground or spoiled in the dishes in which it was placed

The canvas covering the tent gave so little protection that the repast was completely ruined. Probably there were none more keenly disappointed than the boys, as I know from experience, as we expected our hopes were about to be realized.

After the Anti-Masonic excitement had subsided and existed only in memory, the revival of the lodge began to be considered. The causes or necessity for its removal to West Cambridge were given me from some of the members at the time. In the first place, Lexington had been a hotbed in the Anti-Masonic Crusade, and the hatred had been so intense it was feared that there might be influences yet existing that would prevent applications for membership. Also, the Lexington members were so advanced in years that not much assistance in the future could be expected from them. The Cambridge members being younger and willing, if the lodge was transferred to that town, to assume all responsibilities in furnishing the needed requirements, the prospect for accessions for membership was far more assuring.

The strongest argument raised in favor of its removal, and one that could not be controverted, was the old hall. It was poorly arranged, inconvenient, without ante-rooms, and the only entrance was through a sleeping-room. As these obstacles must be remedied, no possible way could be devised.

The location of the Munroe Inn, with its large farm, happened to be particularly favorable for the requirements of the kind of patronage it was receiving at that time; and was so large and lucrative that to reinstate the lodge in the old hall would entail a loss so great to Munroe, by curtailing his already insufficient room, that the expense would exceed the means of the lodge to meet.

Before the advent of railroads, a large portion of the cattle and sheep for the supply of the Brighton market was received mainly from Vermont, New Hampshire and Canada, the animals being driven over the roads in large droves. To make sure of suitable accommodations for the cattle, it was necessary that arrangements be secured in advance, and at such distances as could be reached after each day's drive.

Munroe having a large farm, and it being the last stopping-place before reaching Brighton, the drovers would arrange to reach this place on Saturday and remain until Monday, in order to give the cattle rest and improve their appearance before entering the market. The average cost of feeding the cattle from Saturday to Monday was twenty-five cents per head. It was no unusual occurrence to provide for several hundred cattle for several weeks in succession. Sheep in droves of four or five hundred, and sometimes more, had to be cared for in enclosures as a protection from dogs. The expense of keeping sheep was from five to ten cents each. The revenue at some portions of the year from this source would exceed a hundred dollars per week.

Another source of income for the public houses in town, before the railroads, was the heavy teaming from New Hampshire, Vermont and other places, to and from Boston; some of the teams followed nearly schedule time. Munroe's place was again found especially convenient for this sort of traffic, as they could start from there in the morning, drive to Boston, dispose of their freight and return before night. This custom from teaming made it necessary frequently to use the hall as a sleeping-room, and oftentimes every space available was used for that purpose. It was a common occurrence to stable a hundred horses per night. Incomes from other sources, besides those named, of more or less importance, were received. After mature deliberation it was deemed impracticable to attempt to reinstate the lodge in the old hall.

At the time to which I am referring, there were eleven public houses in Lexington; all were receiving patronage according to their accommodations; three of this number had halls for public use. Six had no land in connection except sufficient for dooryard purposes.

The Munroe farm contained an area of land in extent as large as that of all the other public houses combined. When the Lowell & Fitchburg Railroad commenced running their cars, the stage-coaches soon disappeared, and a reduction in cost of transportation compelled the teaming to be withdrawn. Soon after the diversion of the travel, one after another of the public houses began to close their doors to the public.

Of the eleven houses, two were burned, three were removed, and six now remain and are occupied as private dwellings. The Munroe tavern was probably the first public house opened in Lexington, as there is proof that it existed in 1719, and for fifty-eight years after that time it had several different owners who, in connection with keeping a public house, were engaged in mechanical business. The buildings must have been inadequate for public accommodation, as the house in 1719 was a low-posted, one-story building, and before coming into the possession of William Munroe in 1770 had received several additions.

William Munroe kept the tavern from 1770 to 1815, (forty-five years.) His son Jonas then became the proprietor for thirty-five years. It was, therefore, open to the public 138 years.

As this house was the first one to open its doors for public accommodation in town, and the last of the eleven beforementioned to close them, it is very natural to inquire what prolonged its existence.

Tradition has handed down the report that during the revolutionary struggle, and for several decades afterwards, when the facilities for communication were confined to the mails, and then only received at intervals, the anxiety to obtain the latest information was at times so intense as to be almost unendurable. As a means of receiving as much as possible of the latest news, it became the custom of the male portion of the citizens to meet on evenings at such places as were most convenient, where the thoughts and opinions entertained could be interchanged, and subjects of interest discussed. Col. William Munroe, being a man experienced in military affairs, also prominent in social and trustworthy positions, made his counsel and opinions respected. As his house was conveniently situated, what was at first meeting casually, soon became a common occurrence.

General Washington, when on his visit to Lexington in 1789, was entertained here, which adds another feature of interest to visitors. The locating of Hiram Lodge at the early date of 1797, and its remaining here for twenty-five years, gave it notoriety in a different direction. It can, however, be safely assured, that the affable manner and social disposition of Col. William Munroe, who also seemed to possess an intuitive perception that enabled him to anticipate the wishes of his patrons, were qualifications that made him an ideal landlord. His son, who became his successor as innholder, inherited to a certain degree the traits of his father. The domestic arrangements, free from ostentatious display, the hospitality, and courteous attention, were recognized by the community, as was seen by a continuance of patronage until death removed the proprietor.

A singular custom, that was followed for many years, served to extend the celebrity of this old "Wayside Inn," and the success that William Munroe and his son attained in the preparation of a beverage called "flip" proved to be a profitable factor towards replenishing their exchequer. It was usually made in what was known as a "quart mug." Its component parts were West India rum, sugar, and hop beer; the rum and sugar were selected by exact measurement; then the mug was filled nearly full with beer; the main and absolutely necessary part was given with the loggerhead. This article was of iron, six inches in length and an inch in diameter, tapered at the ends, resembling a cone in shape; a piece of iron, about two feet in length and three-eighths of an inch in diameter, welded to the large piece, served for the handle; the large end, after being heated by placing it in the fire, was dipped in water to remove the ashes, then placed quickly in the mug, and almost immediately a white foam would appear; also a pleasant aroma would greet the senses. This preparation was pleasant to the taste but seductive in effect, especially to a novice in its use, as he would find it more comfortable to be seated than to stand. The demand for this drink in the winter months was so urgent that, to avoid delay, quantities were constantly prepared, with the exception of using the loggerhead, and several of these were kept constantly in the fire.

If there is a spot on this fair land worthy to be retained, and kept in remembrance for what has transpired within its borders, there can be none more entitled to preservation as a historical landmark than the ancient Munroe House.

CHARLES A. WELLINGTON.

EXTRACTS FROM MINUTES, MEETING FEBRUARY 12, 1901.

Remarks of REV. C. A. STAPLES, President of the Society.— Since the last meeting of the Society one of our active and esteemed members has passed away. I refer to Mr. Charles A. Wellington, one of the original members. He was heartily interested in the formation of the Society, constantly attended its meetings, served on many important committees, and gave much time and thought to the promotion of its objects. It seems peculiarly fitting that we should take some action this evening in recognition of our indebtedness for his valuable counsel and unstinted labors in behalf of the Lexington Historical Society, and also of his unselfish spirit and worthy character. Accordingly I have asked his intimate friend, Hon. A. E. Scott, to prepare a suitable expression of our appreciation of his devoted service and of his useful life.

Remarks of HON. A. E. SCOTT.— The Lexington Historical Society mourns the loss of one of its most valued members.

Mr. Charles A. Wellington, who has been connected with our Society since its inception and closely identified with its work, has passed on, leaving a void not only in our organization, but in the town, in our social life and in the home, which it is impossible to fill.

Mr. Wellington passed his whole life in our midst. He was descended from an ancestry that settled in Lexington before its incorporation, participants in the struggle for independence and always prominent in municipal affairs.

Although there was allotted to him a goodly number of

years, with so much of sturdiness and sobriety behind him through so many generations of hardy men added to his own blameless character, it seems to us he might have been spared even through another generation had it not been for the gradual wear and waste of his ever busy life,— his ceaseless activity from early morning often to late night through every day of every year.

His life was one of singular purity. The Golden Rule was the creed that guided him in his dealings with his fellow-men, and with a heart full of true charity he was ever thoughtful of others, forgetful of self.

He always seemed happiest when he was doing something for others or for the public good. He put his whole soul into such work, and we felt safe when he accepted any public responsibility.

He was one of the few men we are always glad to meet. Although often struggling with life's discouragements, he kept his own trials in the background, was ever cheerful in his greetings, always the welcome guest.

He was a man of varied talents, with a capacity for the practical application of his powers seldom equaled.

He was a skilled mechanic, equally at home with the coarser implements of the farm, the intricate machines of the workshop, or the delicate watch.

He had a keen artistic sense,— he had more than this, he was the ideal artist.

His eye was true, his hand was facile. In his hand the graver's chisel wrought exquisite forms, the block of wood became a work of art, the rough quartz an amethyst in beautiful setting. He was equally at home in the office of the architect, in the workshop of the sculptor and in the studio of the painter.

He quickly grasped what was needed for any particular

object, and he was equally quick in the execution of the work. From a piece of sash or a remnant of a door or shutter, or a fragment of a tile, the ancient house is reproduced with historic accuracy and furnished with many appropriate relics. From a bit of old paper found upon its walls is evolved with wonderful patience the intricate pattern a century old.

Under his skillful guidance the picture of the artist is perfected in historic detail, the rough boulders of the field become the artistic fountain,— his own fitting monument, — the hillside glows with its myriad blossoms, the home is replete with utility and beauty.

He was a true naturalist. He loved the fields and the forests, the green meadow with its wealth of flowers, the rugged mountain-side with its mineral treasures. With remarkable keenness of vision he was always the first to discover the rare fern or flower, the crystal or the beryl, the nest of the bird or the animal's track. To him the fox or the deer was a thing to be studied not killed, the crawling reptile or insect was to be avoided not trodden under foot, the moss or the lichen was to be admired and not destroyed.

He was a skilled woodsman, quick to act in emergencies, always doing the right thing at the right time. No precipice so steep but he would find a way to surmount it,— no stream so rapid but he would find a way to cross it,— no storm so sudden or so violent but he would find or construct a shelter,— no night in the forest so dark without the keenest delight by the blazing campfire. A privilege to be always remembered among one's heart treasures to have been with such a man in a forest exploration or on a mountain climb.

His last conscious days were characteristic of his whole

life. He was cheerful and thoughtful, always planning the work there was for him to do and eagerly anticipating the return of health that he might be about it.

Time hastens to dull the memory of the loss of such a man to the community, but the loss to the home must continue to the end, the bitterness of which can only be softened by fond memories of a life full to overflowing with kindness, brilliancy, activity, charity and brotherly love.

His innate modesty kept him from a prominence which his abilities could have commanded, and measured by the standard which the world is prone to set up he was not a great man, but measured by rules of right living, of right acting and of purity of thought, he was one of Nature's noblemen None knew him but to respect him. None knew him intimately but to love him.

Remarks of MR. GEORGE O. SMITH.— I rise to move the adoption of the resolutions offered. From his boyhood I have known Charles Wellington and known him as honest, straightforward, unselfish — as boy and man.

His reserve force and will power were almost miraculous in the accomplishment of whatever he undertook, making him persistent where others would have faltered. An unaffected modesty in regard to his great abilities was a prominent trait in his character.

By cultivation of mind, and the training of his deft fingers in his earlier calling, he exemplified the untruth of the old saying, " knowing all trades and good at none ;" for whether at the jeweler's bench or with the sledge-hammer at the anvil, with the mason's trowel, the plane of the carpenter, the soldering-iron of the plumber or the tin-smith, the tools of the architect, or the pencil or brush of the artist, whatever work left his skillful hands was finished and complete. And not alone was he skillful in mechanic arts. As has been said of another,

> " Great Nature was his Deity:
> In Virtue's temple, firm, unswerved,
> This priest of reason stood and served
> The broad Church of Humanity."

His love of Nature in her differing phases — for rocks and field and woods — was characteristic. He knew and loved the birds and trees, and plants and flowers. Whether for his friends personally or for the public good, no call upon his time and abilities was unanswered, if it were possible for him to grant his services.

On committees of the town and in various ways he has done good and noble work. And not alone in our own town. In the founding of mechanic schools and schools for carving, by Mrs. Hemenway and others, for the benefit of the poorer classes in Boston, his services were availed of, and in our own town in the schools and the several societies beside our own, he has been a willing and untiring worker.

Our Society owes him a lasting debt of gratitude for efforts and work which no other member could have accomplished, in the restoration of the Hancock-Clarke house and in other ways, and as a fellow-member he will be sadly missed.

As tree warden of the town, an office but recently created, we had looked forward to see great benefit from his work and interest in this direction, and here again it will be difficult to fill his place.

Remarks of MR. JAMES P. MUNROE.— I beg to second the resolutions, not because I can say anything which will add in the least to the admiration and respect felt by every one of us for the character of Mr. Charles Wellington, but because it seems to me one of the important duties of such a society as this to honor and to bear conspicuous witness to the lives of such citizens as he. And it is especially appropriate in this instance because to Mr. Wellington in a very unusual measure may be applied the phrase, " a man of antique virtues ;" for he possessed conspicuously the virtues which we associate with the founders of this Republic, without exhibiting any of their unpleasant austerities.

Mr. Wellington was, as you know, a shy man ; but when it was a question of doing good to this town or to any of its citizens, or when it was a question of protecting them from wrong, he was bold as a lion.

He was a reserved man ; but with congenial companions few had so much to say that was worth saying and few could say it half so well.

He was a man, in private conversation, of plain speech and downright sentiments, uncompromising in his judgments ; but this was because he was absolutely honest and single-minded himself and could not tolerate any standard of public and private action less high than his own. What this town and nation need more than anything else is a citizenship more largely made up of such men as Charles A. Wellington.

Remarks of MR. ALBERT S. PARSONS.— Mr. President : It seems hardly safe for me to attempt to say anything after the admirable resolutions which have been offered by Mr. Scott and the appreciative and fitting words which have been said by Mr. Smith and Mr. Munroe. I cannot expect to add anything to the force of these expressions, but I cannot forbear a word of acknowledgment of the respect, esteem and affection which I felt for Mr. Wellington. It was a blessed privilege to have known him. He was the most unselfish man I ever knew. All things considered, I think he was the best man I ever knew. Utterly thoughtless of himself when any opportunity came to serve the town, this society, or any other organization which he felt was working for worthy ends; untiring and self-sacrificing when any friend could be aided; full of zeal for all good works, but with none of the jealousies, or bitterness of feeling, too common with reformers; with only the kindest feelings for every human being and for the animal creation as well; loving Nature in all her aspects and living as closely to her as possible; his life was an example for us all, and I am glad that our tribute to its value is to be put on record.

I hope it can be published in our local papers and widely circulated. Where can we find a nobler example to hold up to our youth? Let no effort be spared to bring home to every young person in Lexington the lesson of his life, — that of devotion to high ideals, to the public good, to adding what one man could to the beauty and the happiness of the world, without a thought of personal gain, of fame, or even of recognition. His excessive modesty and desire to do his work unofficially and unheralded (his only fault) make it the more necessary that we who knew the worth of the man and the great service he was constantly conferring upon the community should bear testimony to the character and the usefulness of his unselfish life.

Permit me a word as to personal knowledge of his abilities in a business way. About a year ago, being suddenly called upon to help save from total wreckage a bankrupt corporation, I asked Mr. Wellington if he would act as a director, — a favor which it troubles my conscience to have asked, for every added duty may have hastened this untimely end. His zeal, industry and interest could not have been greater had his own fortune been at stake. I want to say that if our friend has failed to attain special success in business, I am convinced that it is not from lack of unusual abilities, but because his talents in that direction have been at the service of others, rather than centered upon his own affairs. Had he been so constituted that he could have concentrated the good judgment, the activity and the enterprise which he possessed upon the building up of wealth for himself, he might have won what the world is apt to consider the sole success ; but here, too, is not a life lived for others rather than for self the example young people need in this age of commercialism and greed ?

This society has benefited largely from his labors. Let us see to it that they fail not of recognition by this generation and that they be so recorded that future generations shall realize their debt to this modest, faithful, generous worker.

Further remarks by MR. STAPLES.— I wish to endorse every word that has been spoken of our friend. For nearly twenty years now, I have known him and been associated with him on many town and Society committees. It has been a great pleasure to work with him for objects of mutual interest and the public good. A more unselfish and generous man I have never known. Always ready to help any good cause and giving himself without stint in efficient labors for its progress, no one gave so much time and thought to the saving of the Hancock-Clarke house, restoring its original adornments and making it attractive to thousands of visitors. Some of its valuable relics are his gifts, and the contribution box, and the showcase containing the Governor Dudley pistols and trappings, are fine specimens of his mechanical ingenuity and taste.

The Hayes Fountain, surmounted by its noble statue, is a fitting monument to his unselfish devotion to public duties and interests. He gave much time in superintending its construction, and to his good judgment are largely due its beauty and effectiveness. In the last visit I paid him just before his death, he told me what he meant to do in the spring to improve the grounds around it and make it a still more attractive place. This cherished purpose he fondly dwelt upon in the long hours of pain and weariness and until the end.

I would suggest that this memorial of one so respected and beloved be printed for distribution among our members and his many friends.

The action suggested by Mr. Staples was unanimously approved by a rising vote.

MR. GEORGE O. SMITH.

EXTRACTS FROM MINUTES OF MEETING, FEBRUARY 9, 1904.

Rev. C. A. Staples reported for the committee appointed to take such action on the death of Mr. George O. Smith as was thought best, as follows : At a meeting of the Lexington Historical Society held on Tuesday evening, February 9, 1904, the article in the will of their fellow member, the late George O. Smith, former president and corresponding secretary of the Society, was read, containing its munificent bequest of ten thousand dollars to the Society for certain specific objects, and the following action was proposed :

1st. RESOLVED, that we gratefully accept the bequest of our late honored and beloved associate, Mr. George O. Smith, and pledge ourselves to hold it as a sacred trust, the income to be used in accordance with his desire and his spirit.

2nd. RESOLVED, that a committee on permanent funds consisting of three persons be appointed by the president, who shall receive, invest and hold this bequest when available, and others for a similar object, and make a report of the condition of the same at the annual meeting of the Society, all expenditures from this fund to be first authorized by the Society.

3rd. RESOLVED, that we hereby wish to express and place upon the records the high appreciation in which we hold his bequests to the Society and to the town, and our respect and affection for the memory of our faithful associate, the good citizen, the kind neighbor and the generous friend.

Extract from the Will of Mr. George O. Smith.

To the Lexington Historical Society, if in active being at my decease, five thousand dollars, the income to be expended in historical research for matters pertaining to the efforts of citizens of the Town of Lexington in the Revolutionary period, for the freedom and independence, or for the advancement and welfare of the people of the United States of America and for the publication of the same. After the application of the income for this purpose for fifteen years, if thought best the income may be used for the general purposes of the Society. Should the Society fail to accept or comply with the conditions of this bequest, the amount herein named will be added to the residue of my estate and be disposed of as hereinafter directed.

Extract from Codicil.

If my estate, after payment of debts and expenses, shall net the sum of seventy thousand dollars, the amount of the gift to the Lexington Historical Society shall be increased to ten thousand dollars to be used as in item eleven of my said will.

A Memorial of Mr. George O. Smith.

Among the three hundred and eighty-five men and women who have been connected with the Lexington Historical Society since its organization, no one was more active in promoting its interests and more devoted in attendance upon its meetings than the late George O. Smith, for nearly eight years its corresponding secretary, and its ninth president. His character as a citizen and as a man, not less than his example as a friend and benefactor of the Society, deserves grateful recognition from his fellow members. The respect and affection with which he was regarded by all associated with him make it especially fitting that his memory should be honored and perpetuated in this community, greatly to be benefitted in the future by his wise and generous bequests.

George O. Smith, son of William L. and Hannah (Lane)

Smith, was born in East Lexington, January 5, 1832. His father was a native of Sterling, Mass., and his mother of Bedford, Mass. Her father was a member of the Bedford Company of Minute Men, took an active part in the events of the 19th of April, 1775, and a few years since, Mr. Smith, his grandson, placed a fitting memorial of his service over his grave in the old cemetery at Bedford. George was born in a humble home where rigid economy and hard work were the discipline of the members, and the three children early learned the lesson of self-reliance, so essential to the attainment of any high success or worthy manhood. The only advantages of education afforded him were in the schools of his native village, probably much inferior then to those of the present day. It was always a matter of deep regret to him that he had enjoyed such limited opportunities for intellectual culture, and that he did not have the training in his youth of some higher institution of learning. No doubt the sense of his own deficiencies, and the detriment it was to his usefulness, led him to set aside a large portion of his estate, the income to be devoted to the higher education of young men from the schools of this town.

Early in life Mr. Smith was thrown upon his own resources and learned to make his own way in the world. After various employments in which he won the reputation of being worthy of the fullest confidence of his employers, he began business for himself in a small way, opening a cigar store on Hawley Street in Boston, where the remaining years of his life were passed. As a business man he was universally trusted for undeviating honesty and truth, seeking only that success to be won in doing as he would be done by. His word was as good as his bond. What he told a customer could be relied upon as his honest belief, and what he promised to do that he did, whatever the inconvenience or loss to himself. Justice and sincerity in word and deed, courtesy and kindness in his intercourse with others, fidelity in duty every day, a plain, simple-minded, open-hearted man, making no pretension to wealth, position or learning, content to be known for just what he was and as he was, such was George O. Smith in his business and social relations. And it is worthy of remark that with none of the greed and haste for riches so common in this age, by industry and frugality and good management, wronging none, striving to outstrip none in the race, he accumulated a modest fortune and left more than sixty thousand dollars in public bequests. It shows that the principle of the Golden Rule is not so impracticable in business affairs as some are fond of asserting, but that a fair degree of success is possible without resorting to mean or crooked ways. George O. Smith was not only a man of unimpeachable business integrity and of an honorable success, but of broad sympathies and a generous heart. By his cordial and kindly ways he drew to himself loving and devoted friends wherever he was known. He inspired a confidence and affection which made him a welcome visitor in homes of trouble and sorrow, a trusted guardian of the patrimony of the widow and orphan, a man whose advice and guidance were sought by those beset with discouragement or overcome by adversity. Never did he appear happier than when rendering some service to cheer the hard lot of a sufferer or bearing the burden of some disheartened friend.

In the honor and welfare of Lexington he had a deep and tender interest. Faithful to the duties of a citizen, ready to serve the cause of good government in the town, firm to uphold what he believed to be the principles of righteousness in state and nation, he was a worthy example of the true patriot and servant of the people.

When the first movement was made to form the Lexington Historical Society, Mr. Smith was among its most earnest supporters, and during the years since its organization there have been few meetings when he was not in attendance and an active participant in the proceedings, coming from his temporary home in Somerville even in the coldest and stormiest weather. Of the four papers read by him before the Society, it is but just to say that they are among the most carefully prepared and interesting given at its meetings. His style was singularly simple, clear and direct; he was faithful in his investigations of historic subjects, and related only what he believed to be reliable. It is remarkable that, having so little training in composition at school, and in a life devoted to business pursuits, he attained such accuracy of expression and so large a fund of general information. As corresponding secretary of the Society, there was always manifest a painstaking devotion to his duties. Whatever was given him to do was sure to be done promptly, and he evinced a most conscientious spirit in its minutest details.

The last years of Mr. Smith's life were passed in Somerville, Mass., where he removed after the destruction of the old paternal homestead by the widening of the street. It was a sore experience to him that the home of his childhood and youth, where his parents had lived and died, should be swept away in the ruthless march of modern improvements, but his heart never ceased to yearn for the spot, and thither he was wont often to pass his leisure hours. Here he finally prepared for himself a pleasant home in which to pass the remaining days before he was called to join those who had gone. Mr. Smith had never married. For two years he had been steadily failing and he realized that the end was near, but there was an earnest longing to be settled in his new house that he might die in Lexington. Many times he was heard to express the desire. Then he would say with Simeon of old, " Lord now lettest thou thy servant depart in peace." But it was not to be. He made his last visit to the new house just before his death to see that all was ready for him to keep Thanksgiving Day there, then close at hand. But that festival, so dear to his heart, was kept in a home where the family circle is once more complete. After a very brief illness he passed into the higher life on Monday morning, November 16, 1903. Thus closed a good and noble life which generations to come of the poor, the sick, the suffering of this town, not less than the young men and maidens, "will rise up and call blessed."

At the conclusion of Mr. Staples' report, Mr. Robert P. Clapp made a graceful and feeling tribute to the memory of Mr. Smith, and moved that the memorial, as reported by the committee, be accepted as a matter of record and placed on file, and that it be printed in the next volume of the Proceedings of the Society. The vote was unanimously passed. The resolutions, as reported by the committee, were also unanimously accepted by a rising vote.

Remarks by Mr. James P. Munroe.

(Before Bay State Historical League June 4, 1904.)

To be permitted to translate one's private admiration of a friend into a public appreciation of him before such a gathering as this is indeed a privilege. To attempt to do this when the opportunity presents itself is a pressing duty. Therefore I gladly accept the honor of saying to the Bay

State Historical League a few words, not of fulsome praise, but of simple truth concerning a former President of the Lexington Historical Society who served also as Secretary of this League, Mr. George O. Smith.

I cannot speak of Mr. Smith with the intimacy of a contemporary; for he belonged to a generation earlier than mine. I cannot speak even with the tenderness of one who, as child and boy, grew up at his side; for I did not know him intimately until, about 1890, our common interest in the Lexington Historical Society drew us somewhat closely together. But it is my privilege to speak of him as of one who for a dozen years honored me with a friendship that was almost confidential, and for whom, as his character unfolded itself to me, I felt an ever-deepening affection and an ever-heightening admiration.

It is not easy to expound what we so mistakenly call the "common" virtues, unless they take shape in some uncommon action. It is difficult to draw the portrait of a friend the depth and breadth of whose character it has taken years fully to appreciate. We are so accustomed to interpret men in terms of what they did, that it is not a simple matter to present them in terms of what they were. As many of you know, Mr. Smith's life was quiet, his interests were somewhat limited, his unusual, — indeed his abnormal, — self-depreciation forbade his attempting work that he might easily have done and his occupying positions that he could successfully have filled. As is too often the case with men who have not enjoyed a college education, he overvalued the importance of that training and felt himself handicapped far more than he really was. That through this veil of self-effacement you members of the Historical League who had not previously known him should have perceived so clearly his depth and strength of character conveys to us better than any words of mine the spiritual force of this modest gentleman.

Mr. Smith's father came to Lexington, about 1820, from Stirling, Massachusetts, having at about the same time married Hannah Lane of Bedford, daughter of a soldier of the Revolution. From this marriage there were three children, of whom the youngest, George, was born in 1832. Of alien stock, therefore, George Smith nevertheless loved Lexington with the affection and served her with the fidelity of one whose ancestral roots ran deep down into this sacred soil. And although, as he and many others thought, cruelly injured at her hands, he continued to his last day to lavish upon Lexington a sort of personal affection which in some measure eased, perhaps, the loneliness due to bachelorhood and an unusual dearth of relatives.

As a patriot, Mr. Smith was sound and true; for he held the real meaning of patriotism to be the doing of one's whole duty as a citizen throughout the circle of one's daily life. Were it a question of politics, he voted as he honestly believed. Were it a question of town affairs, he seldom failed in attendance upon public meetings, he never failed in the performance of whatever work his fellow-citizens appointed him to do. Were it a question of the church, he served the parish of East Lexington, during many years, with zeal and with fidelity. And, finally, were it a question of human relationships, of the administering of trust funds, of the helping of friends in distress, of the furthering of young men in business, of the giving of advice and comfort out of the stores of his experience, George Smith never demurred, never slackened for a moment his vigilence or his interest, always showed himself to be ready to listen, to be patient with broken promises, to be tolerant even of that imposture which is ever trying to over-reach such crystal honesty as his. He was as stern toward himself as any Puritan; he was as sympathetic toward others as any minister of Christ. His loneliness, his regret at not having had larger opportunities, his private griefs, his indignation at the sweeping away of his home before the march of so-called progress, made him perhaps, a little embittered towards life, but they did not make him uncharitable; he did not seize upon these as excuses for not doing his full duty to society. But I think it may fairly be said that most of the great amount of work for others which George Smith did, had its foundation in a high sense of duty rather than in any joy in altruism. Certainly that service was not done for emolument, for he was as generous with money as with time; most assuredly it was not done through vanity, for he shrank from any form of praise. One kind of service, however, he performed with eagerness, with wholeheartedness, with almost boyish zeal, — and that was his work for your League and for our Historical Society. That labor was done because he loved it, because he delighted, as only the true historian can take pleasure, in rescuing from oblivion every least fact of history, in shedding light upon every smallest step in the progress of Lexington or of these United States. No act of the Lexington Historical Society, from its inception twenty years ago far into that future which this bequest will make so much more fruitful for it, but was of the greatest moment and of the keenest consequence to him. Equally, every step in the formation and progress of your League engaged his closest and, as you know, his most sympathetic and helpful interest. And, finally, when death came so unexpectedly, taking him away just as he was to come back to Lexington — for although his legal residence and all his interests were here, he had lived for a number of years in Somerville — we found that he had made large provision in his will for the carrying on of that work in history which had been the absorbing avocation of his later years. That will, moreover, created other admirable trusts, the most notable being one which, generation after generation, and in a most wise way, will encourage Lexington young men to seek that higher education the lack of which the testator himself so keenly felt. In death, then, as in life, Mr Smith's unassuming but strong personality will be felt here and elsewhere, aiding ambitous youth, comforting the afflicted, encouraging patriotism by stimulating the study of our nation's history.

When the names of men who now seem greater than Mr. Smith shall have faded into oblivion, the quiet influence of this man who shrank even from friendly notice, will be steadily spreading; and it will be building up, we feel sure, other such lives as his, — lives of absolute integrity, of never-failing courtesy, of helpfulness to others, of devotion to town and church and state, of silent but deep enthusiasm for all those things, in the past and in the present, which make men strong and true, useful and really happy.

Remarks by Mr. Robert P. Clapp.

Mr. President: It is well that a society like this should record, from time to time, as they pass on to a higher sphere of action, memorials of such persons as have in some conspicuous degree deserved well of the community in which they lived. The duty in this regard which the present occasion puts upon us, is one that we perform with sadness, for he who has gone so suddenly away was endeared to us all by his kindly qualities and strong personal charms. But the feeling is tempered well with pride and satisfaction, since the record which he leaves behind is one that does credit to this town, and furnishes an inspiration to every one who would lead a high-minded, unselfish and useful life.

Though not my good fortune to have known Mr. Smith closely as a friend or neighbor, I have been many times an associate of his upon committees and have in other ways seen enough of him to be impressed by the gentleness and refinement, sympathy, cheerfulness, fidelity, and high moral courage which had their abode in the man ; and so, though I cannot add anything to the just and discriminating memorial which has been read, I am unable to refrain from adding my word of tribute to his worth.

His life has been, it seems to me, one illustrating the heroism of peace. It has been said that "dissatisfaction with life's endeavor springs in some degree from dullness;" that "we require higher tasks because we do not recognize the height of those we have;" that "trying to be kind and honest seems an affair too simple and too inconsequential for gentlemon of our heroic mould;" and so "we had rather set ourselves to something bold, arduous and conclusive." Our friend, however, had the wisdom to recognize the height of his tasks, and to see that being honest and kind, living a simple, frugal life, serving with attentive kindness his friends and neighbors, performing with quiet dignity and unselfishness the duties of a citizen, and husbanding his resources for the ultimate benefit of humanity in his native town, was an undertaking worthy of daily and lifelong patience and fortitude.

A man's personal traits may sometimes be well estimated from the character of his will and testament. In the case of our friend this fact is illustrated with uncommon effect, for the paper was drawn with his own hand, apparently unaided by anyone. Having comparatively little legal terminology, and being written in his own literary style — a style, as you well know, possessed of much merit — the document reflects his individual qualities and makes clear his aspirations. A copy should be filed in the archives of this society. I will refer to one clause, characteristic of the fine spirit pervading the whole instrument. To a certain person he gives the sum of $500 "as a recognition," so the text runs, "of my appreciation of the legatee's devotion to his mother, in whose family I lived for many years, and of a long period of friendship unclouded by the slightest unpleasantness." The will breathes a spirit of service for others, and shows his devotion to the interests of this society and his love for Lexington.

As I think of this beautiful life, so fruitful in good deeds, and so satisfying in the rewards of service to him who has done them, and note the completeness of endeavor with which his day has ended, I am reminded of the memorial verse:

> " A late lark twitters in the quiet skies;
> And from the west,
> Where the sun, his day's work ended,
> Lingers as in content,
> There falls on the old, gray city
> An influence luminous and serene,
> A shining peace.
>
> " The smoke ascends
> In a rosy-and-golden haze. The spires
> Shine, and are changed. In the valley
> Shadows rise. The lark sings on. The sun,
> Closing his benediction,
> Sinks, and the darkening air
> Thrills with a sense of the triumphing night —
> Night with her train of stars
> And her great gift of sleep.

"So be my passing!
My task accomplished and the long day done,
My wages taken, and in my heart
Some late lark singing,
Let me be gathered to the quiet west,
The sundown splendid and serene."

REV. CARLTON A. STAPLES.

BY CHARLES FRANCIS CARTER, *President.*

An appreciation of the life and character of the Rev. Carlton A. Staples finds most appropriate setting in the records of the Lexington Historical Society. For in the fellowship of its gatherings around the genial glow of the wood blazing in the old fireplace, those qualities appeared in free, unmistakable emphasis that denoted the man as he was and had been in all the relations of life. There was a singular simplicity about him and a manifest continuity of character from the early years until the last. Those who knew the boy might have accurately prophesied the man, while those who knew the man could easily guess what the boy had been. He peculiarly exemplified the phrase used of another,—"the boy conserved in the man."

To five parishes he had ministered before coming to Lexington. Whether in Meadville or St. Louis, in the years before the Civil War, in Milwaukee, Chicago or Providence, he was the earnest, whole-souled man we knew him to be here, giving himself in free-handed, generous service and hearty good-will to all about him. When we think of him as chaplain in the army, identifying himself with the Union cause and finding his parish in the camp and on the field, we need not to be told of the ready sympathy he brought to the suffering, the manly tenderness and true counsel, for these were part of the man, whether in the thirties or the seventies. And he who spoke to the members of the Grand Army Post with such glowing fervor and who shared the solemn exercises of Memorial Day with such keen appreciation would have been a comrade in spirit even if he had not also been one in fact.

Those who have heard him take part in town meeting, ever earnest and often vehement, never using words for oratorical effect but always to make his meaning and convictions clear, uncompromising whenever a question of principle was involved and ardently seeking the good of the community—those who have thus witnessed his devotion to the town know that wherever he might have been he would have been a public-spirited man, always to be depended on to take his part and to stand for the right. As trustee of Cary Library and chairman of the board for thirteen years, he rendered admirable service to the town, being zealous to raise the standard of literary interest and to extend the use of the library as widely as possible. His impatience with the trivial and his scorn for the flashy often added to the humor of the situation when books were under discussion with his fellow trustees, and the quick vent given to petty prejudices was passed with a smile, for these foibles were the manifest foil of finer traits and carried their own antidote with them.

A rare citizen and a true minister, who will deny that his public life found its freest expression within the field of Lexington's history, that never lost for him its charm and inspiration? Identified with the Society from the first and associated with the Rev. Edward G. Porter in its organization, he gave himself unstintedly to further its interests, and the more he gave the more he received. Where in our midst has been a finer instance of the truth of the great paradox that the life lost is the life saved? It was so manifestly a service of love he rendered, yet for his own sake who would have had it less complete, for this service was to him a perennial spring of joy? Blessed is the man who has an absorbing interest!

As president of the Society for several years and as its

historian, he guided and shaped its development. His name appears oftener than that of any other on its records, and his pen has furnished many valuable pages to the chronicles of the olden time. The most conspicuous work he did was the saving of the Hancock-Clarke house. In the year 1896 preparations were being made to tear down the old house in which the Rev. John Hancock and the Rev. Jonas Clarke had lived, to which Hancock and Adams had often resorted for safety and consultation, which had also been one chief objective of Revere's midnight ride and a center of influence in those stirring times. Standing on its original site, it was not for sale. It would have been an everlasting pity, a calamity that makes one shudder now to think of, had the old house been destroyed. Yet such things happen and no one speaks until the time for action has gone by. Then comes lasting regret. Fortunately for Lexington and for the United States of America, there was a man here who felt what the passing of this landmark would mean. He saw that it must be preserved. He stirred the citizens to action and initiated a movement to secure the needful funds. He agreed to buy the house, pledging his own resources, while depending on the growing spirit and good faith of the community. He effected the trade and the house was moved from its foundation to a new site just across the way, facing the street at the same angle as before but exactly reversed. It was repaired and strengthened in the framework, and now as the home of the Society is the repository of its valuable relics, that have come to it in surprising numbers because of such a permanent home, and a Mecca for thousands of patriotic pilgrims who yearly come to it from all parts of the world. In the preservation of this house a monument has been erected that should so long as it endures, be associated with the name of Mr. Staples.

If the house is now, in some true sense, his monument, while he was living he made the past to glow within it as no other could. How vivid the past became as he rehearsed the story! His was not the detached interest of an antiquary who gathers fossil forms from a dead past, that one may whet his curiosity upon them. In the relics he felt the pulse of the living past and was transported to it, and his talk about it transported those who heard. Hence the rare delight it was to make the round of the chambers with him and share the knowledge and feeling that were deeper still.

From the old parsonage to the village green is a short walk. It took our friend to the place he loved best in this whole world. Who that has seen him there, telling the story he knew and loved so well, can ever forget the picture and the impression of it? Going to the monument, with the gesture of a parish priest, he would gather the people around him, disposing them as he would that they might see and hear, and then, his face aglow, his voice vibrant with the theme, his being suffused with the spirit of it, he would tell of the British and the minutemen on that April day big with destiny, while his own person in form and feature seemed a present embodiment of the stalwart heroism enacted on that green so long ago. To have seen and heard him there was to have an ineffaceable impression of a great event in history.

Thus in all the relations he sustained there appeared the virtues of a spontaneous nature: sympathy and enthusiasm. As was said of Dr. Arnold of Rugby, he was *totus in illo*. The whole man went into everything he did. Things interested him very much or not at all. There was never any doubt as to the genuineness of his feelings and his expression of them. When associated with other speakers in public, one could readily tell the impression being made on him, as the half-suppressed sigh indicated his dissent or wonder how anybody could say such a thing as that, while his entire bearing, when in agreement, would show most cordial satisfaction. He had almost the mind of a child in the completeness of surrender to whatever appealed to him, and, because it meant so much to him, with something of the same childlike spirit he wanted to tell about it and to share it with others. This gave to his personality a charm that will bring many a smile of gladness to those who recall his hearty way. In his sympathy there was a kind of eagerness that made you sure of it beforehand, and whether he was admitting you to a share in his life, the last good story he had heard, or some deeper concern, or whether he was entering into your need, your joy or sorrow, you felt he was giving you the genuine fellowship of a whole-souled man.

Through the possession of these qualities appeared what was perhaps the most distinctive trait in his character that more nearly than anything else accounts for the influence he had. Whatever he had was freely available for use. He filled a large place in the community, not because of extraordinary endowments, but because all that he was he freely rendered for others' good. Here was no hoarded manhood. All the talents were put out at interest, and his fellow-men were the beneficiaries, while on the score of his life was written, *Con amore*, and in the sharing of it he had rare and constant joy.

THE REV. CARLTON A. STAPLES.

RESOLUTIONS OFFERED BY MR. JAMES P. MUNROE AT A MEETING HELD OCTOBER 11, 1904.

At the close of fifty years of devoted and successful ministry and of fruitful citizenship, at the golden milestone of a blessed married life, the Reverend Carlton A. Staples has been translated, without pain, suffering or weakness, to another life.

No other ending of such a beneficent life could be so fitting; but no other death in Lexington could so bereave the town. As a minister he preached the Christian virtues, he taught simplicity of living, he exhorted his people to love and serve their fellow-men. As a man he never failed to exemplify those virtues, that simplicity, such unflagging love and service. As a citizen he showed us, old and young, what true citizenship means. As an historian and speaker he taught us to appreciate the real greatness of what our fathers did, the high measure of our obligation to their heroism. As a preserver of this Hancock-Clarke House, he built a new shrine for eager pilgrims, a new altar whereon the thousands who make this pilgrimage may pledge themselves to the service of a genuine patriotism. As a member, as the historian, and as president of this Society, he was the heart that sent life through its arteries, giving the organization vitality and insuring to it enduring activity.

Recognizing these and many other noble and rare qualities in Mr. Staples, we of the Lexington Historical Society desire to put on record our gratitude that this town, for twenty-three years, has been blessed with such a power for good as he. We desire to express our appreciation, moreover, of his extraordinary services to this organization through his zeal as a member, through his learning as an historian, and through his power as a writer and speaker. Especially do we wish to acknowledge his illuminating papers prepared for this Society, his careful records as its historian, his tireless hospitality in welcoming and instructing the thousands of visitors, and his generous labors in connection with the preservation, restoration and care of this Hancock-Clarke House.

Finally, as men and women who mourn with them, we would respectfully convey to his wife and son our profound sympathy in a loss the greatness of which, in all its phases, only they can fully understand.

Additional remarks were also made by Mr. A. S. Parsons.

PROCEEDINGS.

REGULAR MEETING, December 12, 1899.

A commitee was appointed to have charge of literary exercises at approaching celebration of April 19th.

Rev. James Benton Werner read a paper upon "A Pennsylvania German Village."

The president announced that the Society would observe Forefathers' Day on December 20, and Prof. John Fiske would deliver an address in Hancock Church on "The Salem Witchcraft."

SPECIAL MEETING, January 9, 1900.

A committee of five was appointed to consider plans for celebrating the fourteenth anniversary of the formation of the Society. The Society voted to have the annual meeting accompanied by a banquet.

Rev. C. A. Staples was made delegate to a special anniversary meeting of the Worcester Antiquarian Society.

Dr. W. O. Perkins read a paper on "Latin and Anglo-Saxon Types of Civilization."

REGULAR MEETING, February 13, 1900.

The president announced the death of Rev. Edward G. Porter and appointed a committee of five to suggest suitable action in regard to it. The committee reported later, through Rev. C. A. Staples, an appreciative testimonial to Mr. Porter and his valuable services to the Society, which report the meeting accepted and directed it spread upon the records.

Miss Mary E. Hudson read a paper entitled "Some Memories of the Lexington Centennial."

ANNUAL MEETING, March 13, 1900.

The Society held a banquet in Old Belfry Club House, with appropriate speeches. The business meeting was adjourned to March 20.

ADJOURNED ANNUAL MEETING, March 20, 1900.
The regular annual reports were made and accepted.
The following officers were elected for the ensuing year:
President, Rev. Carlton A. Staples.
Vice-Presidents, Mr. George O. Whiting, Mr. Everett M. Mulliken, Mr. Frank C. Childs, Miss Mary E. Hudson, Miss M. Alice Munroe.
Recording Secretary, Mr. Irving P. Fox.
Corresponding Secretary, Mr. George O. Smith.
Treasurer, Mr. Leonard A. Saville.
Historian, Rev. C. A. Staples.
Custodian, Mr. Charles A. Wellington.
The council appointed, as house committee for the year: Mr. C. A. Wellington, Rev. C. A. Staples, Mr. George O. Whiting, Mrs. A. S. Parsons, Mr. C. B. Davis, Miss M. Alice Munroe.

REGULAR MEETING, April 10, 1900.
Mr. E. P. Nichols read a paper on the "Life and Character of Edward Everett."

REGULAR MEETING, October 9, 1900.
Resolutions on the death of Rev. Cyrus Hamlin, D. D., presented with some interesting personal recollections by Rev. A. W. Stevens, were unanimously adopted.
The committee on Hancock-Clarke House reported that ten thousand people had visited the house during the last six months.
A committee was appointed to consider some means of better protecting the Old Belfry from the elements and from relic-hunters.
Mr. Staples reported, informally, on the search for graves of British soldiers killed at the Battle of Lexington.
Dr. Francis H. Brown read an interesting and suggestive paper on "The Aims and Objects of our Patriotic Societies."
Mr. Charles A. Wellington resigned his office as custodian and Mr. Charles B. Davis was chosen for the unexpired term.

REGULAR MEETING, December 9, 1900.
President Staples read a letter from the Deliverance Munroe Chapter, D. A. R., asking that the Historical Society take charge of a tablet

the chapter had recently placed on the Munroe house facing Common.

Mr. Edward P. Bliss read a paper on his recent tour through Greece.

SPECIAL MEETING, January 15, 1901.

A resolution of sympathy with our fellow-member, Mr. Charles A. Wellington, in his distressing and critical illness, was unanimously adopted.

Mr. Staples read a short paper upon "Lexington One Hundred Years Ago and Lexington To-day," after which Mr. Abram English Brown of Bedford read a paper upon "Peter Faneuil and His Gifts to Boston."

REGULAR MEETING, February 12, 1901.

The president feelingly referred to the recent death of Mr. Charles A. Wellington, one of the original and most active members of the Society, and was followed by Hon. A. E. Scott, Mr. George O. Smith, Mr. James P. Munroe and Mr. A. S. Parsons, in warm tribute to Mr. Wellington's worth.

By a rising vote the meeting unanimously approved the suggestion that the remarks be spread upon the records and printed and sent to Mr. Wellington's family.

A letter from Mrs. Van Ness was read, asking that the Society take measures toward putting the Old Cemetery in repair.

It was voted to ask for insertion in the next town warrant of an article asking for an appropriation for this purpose.

Mr. Robert P. Clapp read a paper on his recent experiences in Constantinople.

ANNUAL MEETING, March 12, 1901.

The usual annual reports were read and accepted.

The following officers were elected for the ensuing year:

President, Rev. Carlton A. Staples.

Vice-Presidents, Mr. Edward P. Bliss, Mr. E. A. Bayley, Mrs. J. O. Tilton, Miss E. M. Tower, Mr. Charles H. Wiswell.

Recording Secretary, Mr. Irving P. Fox.

Treasurer, Mr. L. A. Saville.

Historian, Rev. C. A. Staples.

Custodian, Dr. F. S. Piper.
Corresponding Secretary, Mr. George O. Smith.
House Committee, Mr. George O. Whiting, Mrs. W. H. Greeley, Rev. C. F. Carter, Rev. C. A. Staples, Mrs. H. H. Putnam, A. C. Washburn.
Committee on Publication, Mr. James P. Munroe, Mr. A. S. Parsons, Rev. C. A. Staples, Miss M. E. Hudson, Mr. Irving P. Fox.

Voted that a photograph of the late Charles A. Wellington be framed and placed in the Hancock-Clarke House.

In place of a paper the president read extracts from an unpublished book by Edward Burnham, entitled, "What Edward Burnham Saw at the Hancock-Clarke House."

REGULAR MEETING, April 9, 1901.

The paper of the evening, a "Study of the Works of William Makepeace Thackeray" was read by Rev. Charles J. Staples of Manchester.

REGULAR MEETING, October 8, 1901.

The custodian presented a full report showing the difficult and painstaking work done in arranging, labeling and indexing the possessions of the Society.

The House Committee reported that from April 16 to October 1 the house was visited by nearly 11,000 persons.

President Staples read a paper written by the late Francis Brown, giving recollections of the early ministers of Lexington.

SPECIAL MEETING, November 12, 1901.

Rev. James Salloway of Bedford read a paper on Cotton Mather.

REGULAR MEETING, December 10, 1901.

Rev. Charles F. Carter gave an address upon the recent Yale Bi-Centennial.

REGULAR MEETING, February 11, 1902.

The paper of the evening was by Mr. Albert W. Bryant upon "The Anti-Masonic Movement in the United States and particularly in Lexington."

In the absence of Mr. Bryant, now eighty-eight years of age, his paper was read by Dr. F. S. Piper.

ANNUAL MEETING, March 11, 1902.

Banquet at Old Belfry Club House. Mr. James P. Munroe read a paper upon "Shays' Rebellion."

The business meeting was adjourned to March 18.

ADJOURNED ANNUAL MEETING, March 18, 1902.

The annual reports were made and accepted.

The following officers were elected for the ensuing year:

President, Mr. George O. Smith.

Vice-Presidents, Rev. C. F. Carter, Mr. F. C. Childs, Mr. Hammon Reed, Miss E. S. Parker, Miss E. E. Harrington.

Recording Secretary, Mr. Irving P. Fox.

Treasurer, Mr. L. A. Saville.

Historian, Rev. C. A. Staples.

Custodian, Dr. F. S. Piper.

Corresponding Secretary, Mr. George O. Smith.

House Committee, Mr. George O. Whiting, Rev. C. A. Staples, Mr. A. C. Washburn, Mr. A. Bradford Smith, Miss M. Alice Munroe, Mrs. Ellen B. Lane.

Committee on Publication, Mr. James P. Munroe, Mr. A. S. Parsons, Rev. C. A. Staples, Miss M. E. Hudson, Mr. Irving P. Fox.

Mr. Staples read an extract from the "Life of Henry Ware, Jr.," describing the former occupant of the Hancock-Clarke House, Rev. Jonas Clarke, and his family.

REGULAR MEETING, April 8, 1902.

Rev. C. A. Staples read a most interesting paper upon "The Origin and Extinction of Slavery in Massachusetts."

REGULAR MEETING, October 14, 1902.

A committee of five was appointed to consider the matter of providing better protection for the valuable possessions of the Society.

Dr. Francis H. Brown read a paper on "The Old Burial Ground." Over seven hundred epitaphs had been deciphered and transcribed.

REGULAR MEETING, January 13, 1903.

The meeting of the Society, December 9, 1902, was prevented by a disastrous fire in the immediate vicinity of the Hancock-Clarke House. President Smith had placed in the house a large hand loom, and a lady was present to show how cloth was woven in the olden time, but the whole matter was indefinitely postponed.

The meeting January 13, 1903, was held in the Hancock-Clarke House.

The House Committee reported that 14,290 persons had visited the house between April 1 and December 1, 1902.

President Smith feelingly referred to the recent death of Mr. Albert W. Bryant, one of the Society's oldest and most interested members, and a committee was appointed to prepare suitable resolutions.

The paper of the evening was by Rev. C. A. Staples, on "Massachusetts in the Colonial Period."

REGULAR MEETING, February 10, 1903.

Mr. Staples, for committee, reported appropriate resolutions on the death of Mr. Albert W. Bryant.

Mr. A. Bradford Smith read a paper on "The Old Concord Turnpike," and Miss Elizabeth W. Harrington followed with a paper upon "Early Clock-making in Lexington."

Mr. Nichols gave an interesting explanation of the derivation of the name "Trapelo," in connection with Trapelo Road.

ANNUAL MEETING, March 10, 1903.

The annual reports were read and accepted.

The following officers were chosen for the ensuing year:

President, Rev. Charles F. Carter.

Vice-Presidents, Mr. Hammon Reed, M r. Frank C. Childs, Mr

Charles G. Kauffman, Miss Elizabeth S. Parker. Miss Ellen E. Harrington.
Recording Secretary, Mr. Irving P. Fox.
Treasurer, Mr. Leonard A. Saville.
Historian, Rev. C. A. Staples.
Custodian, Dr. F. S. Piper.
Corresponding Secretary, Mr. George O. Smith.
House Committee, Mr. George O. Whiting, Rev. C. A. Staples, Mr. A. C. Washburn, Mr. Cornelius Wellington, Miss M. Alice Munroe, Mrs. Ellen B. Lane.
Committee on Publication, Mr. James P. Munroe, Mr. Albert S. Parsons, Rev. C. A. Staples, Miss Mary E. Hudson, Mr. Irving P. Fox.

The paper was read by Mrs. David W. Muzzey on "Colonial Industries."

On motion of Mr. Nichols it was voted that the secretary be instructed to request our representative in the Legislature to take such action as, in his judgment, might seem best, to secure for the Society the drum used on Lexington Green April 19, 1775, and now in the State House in Boston.

REGULAR MEETING, April 14, 1903.

Mr. George O. Smith reported his attendance, as delegate, at the meeting of the newly formed Bay State Historical League. On motion of Mr. Clapp it was voted that the Lexington Historical Society join the Bay State Historical League.

Mr. Herbert G. Locke read a paper on "Recent 19th of April Celebrations."

REGULAR MEETING, October 13, 1903.

The House Committee reported that the number of visitors at the old house from April 1 to October 10, 1903, was 18,855.

The amendment to the By-Laws proposed at the last meeting, that Article III., third paragraph, be so amended as to read, "Each member shall pay an admission fee of $1.00 and an annual assessment of 50 cents after the year of admission," was taken from the table and passed without a dissenting vote.

Miss Mary E. Hudson read a paper entitled "Early Days of the Lexington High School."

REGULAR MEETING, December 8, 1903.

President Carter announced to the Society the death of Mr. George O. Smith. Appreciative remarks followed from Mr. R. P. Clapp and Mr. James P. Munroe. A committee of three was appointed to draft suitable resolutions to be placed upon the records of the Society.

Mr. A. S. Parsons, one of the executors, read articles from the will of Mr. Smith, in which $10,000 is given to this Society.

The House Committee reported that 20,255 persons had visited the house and signed the register during the year, and over $1,000 had been received in contributions from visitors.

Mr. M. J. Canavan read a paper on "The Old Main Road in Lexington, with Particular Attention to the Settlement around the Common."

Mr. James P. Munroe presented, with appropriate remarks, three medals which had been conferred upon the late Baroness von Olnhausen by the German Emperor, in recognition of her services as an army nurse. One of the medals, the Iron Cross, has been given to no other American woman except Miss Clara Barton, the head of the Red Cross Society.

The Society voted that a tablet be prepared, in memory of Baroness von Olnhausen, and placed in some prominent position in the Hancock-Clarke House.

REGULAR MEETING, February 9, 1904.

Rev. C. A. Staples, for the committee appointed to take action on the death of Mr. George O. Smith, reported suitable resolutions and read a memorial of Mr. Smith which was followed by a graceful and feeling tribute from Mr. Robert P. Clapp.

The Society voted that the resolutions, which were accepted by a rising vote, and the memorial prepared by Mr. Staples, be placed on file and be printed in the next volume of the Proceedings of the Society.

The reading of the paper announced for this meeting was postponed till a later date.

ANNUAL MEETING, March 8, 1904.

The president announced that he had appointed as the committee to represent the Society in relation to the bequest of the late Mr.

Smith, Mr. George O. Whiting, Mr. Robert P. Clapp and Mr. E. P. Nichols. Dr. F. S. Piper, retiring custodian, made an extended report, and on motion of Rev. Mr. Staples it was voted that "the thanks of the Society be extended to Dr. Piper for his most able and conscientious services and great fidelity as custodian during his term of office covering about three years."

Voted: That Vols. I. and II. of the Proceedings of the Society be offered for sale to members of the Society at 50 cents each. Dr. Piper, Miss Hudson and Miss Kirkland were appointed a committee to investigate the authenticity of the relics in possession of the Society; also to coöperate with trustees of Cary Library with view to making publications received by the Society more accessible to the public.

Voted: That a banquet be held in connection with the April meeting.

Voted: That invitation be extended to the Bay State Historical League to hold its annual outing in Lexington June 4. The chair appointed Rev. Mr. Staples, Miss M. Alice Munroe and Mrs. W. C. Stickle a committee on reception.

The following officers were elected:
President, Rev. Charles F. Carter.
Vice-Presidents, Mr. H. Reed, Mr. F. C. Childs, Mr. Charles G. Kauffman, Miss E. S. Parker, Miss E. E. Harrington.
Recording Secretary, Mr. Irving P. Fox.
Treasurer, Mr. L. A. Saville.
Historian, Rev. C. A. Staples.
Custodian, Miss Marion P. Kirkland.
Corresponding Secretary, Miss Mary E. Hudson.
House Committee, Mr. G. O. Whiting, Rev. C. A. Staples, Mr. A. C. Washburn, Mr. Cornelius Wellington, Miss M. A. Munroe, Mrs. E. B. Lane.
Committee on Publication, Mr. J. P. Munroe, Mr. A. S. Parsons, Rev. C. A. Staples, Miss M. E. Hudson, Mr. Irving P. Fox.

Miss Mary E. Hudson read an interesting account from a letter written by herself on June 18, 1875, descriptive of the visit of General W. T. Sherman to Lexington at that time. The Rev. Mr. Staples read a short sketch narrating how the Hancock-Clarke House was saved and purchased by the Society.

MEETING, April 12, 1904.

This meeting was in the form of a banquet served at the Old Belfry Club House, at which about one hundred members and friends were present. The members of the committee having it in charge were: Rev. C. A. Staples, Mr. J. F. Russell, Miss M. Alice Munroe, Mrs. F. C. Childs and Mr. H. W. Porter.

An oration was delivered by Mr. Edwin D. Mead on "The Evolution of Peace." Mr. Robert P. Clapp also spoke. Mrs H. W. Porter, Miss Mabel Stroch and Miss Alice Williams furnished a musical programme.

REGULAR MEETING, October 11, 1904.

The treasurer announced the bequest of $3,000 to the Society from the estate of the late Mr. Billings of Boston and the gift was accepted. Mr. Piper was authorized to examine grave in Old Cemetery supposed to contain remains of British soldier and, if satisfied of the truth of the tradition, to place a marker upon the spot.

The death of the Rev. Carlton A. Staples, a former president of the Society and its historian from the time of its formation until his death, was formally announced by the president.

Mr. James P. Munroe read a tribute to the memory of Mr. Staples, which will be found in the former part of this volume. After additional remarks by the president and Mr. A. S. Parsons, the tribute was unanimously accepted, all standing, as expressing the sentiment of the Society.

A committee was appointed — Mr. J. P. Munroe, Miss Hudson and Mr. Nichols — to secure a portrait of Mr. Staples, to be hung in the Hancock-Clarke House, bearing an inscription calling particular attention to his efforts in the preservation of the house. It was also voted that this committee prepare and publish a suitable memorial leaflet.

It was voted that the house be kept open throughout the winter, notwithstanding the slight financial loss.

Dr. F. S. Piper was appointed historian and member of House Committee in the place of the late Mr. Staples, and Rev. C. F. Carter, member of Publication Committee.

A paper upon the "Munroe Tavern," written by the late Albert W. Bryant, was read by Dr. Piper.

REGULAR MEETING, December 13, 1904.

The president announced that during the summer he had prepared large photographs, 4 x 5 feet, of the Captain Parker statue and of the Hancock-Clarke House, and that they had been exhibited in the Massachusetts House during the Louisiana Purchase Exposition, that they would also be on exhibition at the Oregon Fair, that the total expense had not exceeded $50, and that his action had been approved by the council.

Mr. A. Bradford Smith read a short sketch of a British officer who was found lying dead on the doorstep of his grandfather's house on the day of the battle. This step is the same as is now in use before the Hancock-Clarke House.

Mr. Arthur E. Horton, C. E., read a suggestive paper on the " First Settlements of Lexington," which was followed by a discussion by members.

GIFTS.

Framed photographs of portraits of Thomas Hancock, Lydia Hancock, his wife, and John Hancock. Given by Mrs. Lydia B. Taft.

Table from Dr. Clarke's house, skillet and two brass kettles. Loaned by Mrs. Lydia B. Taft.

Engraving, " First Reading of Emancipation Proclamation Before the Cabinet." Pitcher used in the Byam family for more than one hundred years. Both given by Mrs. E. M. Byam.

More than fifty articles, including books, sermons, pictures, bedstead, etc. From the estate of Miss Sarah Chandler.

Two spinning-wheels, reel and pudding-dish. From Mrs. Sophia Davis and Mrs. Mary Meserve.

Letters of Chris. Kilby to Thomas Hancock, Arkansas treasury warrants, Confederate money. Given by Mrs. G. Mears.

Dedham Hist. Register, Vols. X. and IV. Given by Dedham Hist. Society.

Worcester Society of Antiquity, 1898. Given by Worcester Society of Antiquity.

Grapeshot from Mt. Independence, Ticonderoga, 1777. Bullet from Plains of Abraham, Sept. 13, 1759. A true piece of Plymouth Rock. Button of British soldier taken from trench on Bunker Hill. Fragment of blood-stained cloth taken from one of the minute men of Cambridge, April 19, 1775. Photograph of Vane made in 1721 and placed on the New Brick Hanover Street Church. Pamphlet memorial to the men of Cambridge who fell in the first battle of the Revolutionary war. All given by Mr. W. A. Saunders of Cambridge.

Framed list of Americans killed April 19, 1775. Given by Mr. E. W. McGlenen.

Complete alphabetical index of all guests at Centennial dinner, April 19, 1875, with number of seat occupied by each. From Miss Mary E. Hudson.

Original manuscript draft, framed, of the first call, signed by Rev. E. G. Porter and Rev. C. A. Staples, preliminary to the formation of the Society. From Mr. H. G. Locke.

GIFTS. xiii.

Twenty photographs of places of historic interest. Papers relating to inmates of Clarke House. Brittannia lamps and bakers. Bill of Stephen Paddock against John Hancock, 1769. Log book of Ship Bombay, a paper published during the War of 1812, and a Federalist. All from Mrs. C. C. Goodwin.

Powder-horn found by the late L. G. Babcock on the battlefield of Port Hudson. From Mrs. Babcock.

Silhouette of Mary, eldest daughter of Rev. Jonas Clarke. From Mrs. Lucy Clarke Powers of Lansingburg, N. Y., granddaughter of the original of the picture.

Winnowing basket of ancient use; two calashes. Poem by Rev. John Pierpont, and one by Hannah F. Gould, sung at the ceremony attending removal of the bones of the minute men from the Old Burying-ground to the Common in 1835. Sermon by Jonas Clarke preached in 1770. Proclamation of Gov. John Hancock relating to Shays' Rebellion, 1787. All from Mrs. Howland Holmes.

Knife and canteen picked up on one of the battlefields of the Civil War. From Mr. George W. Field of Lowell.

Additional volume containing names of Massachusetts soldiers and sailors who served in the Revolution. From the Commonwealth of Massachusetts.

Handsome mahogany cabinet formerly used in the Hancock-Clarke House, and in which state papers of great value were hidden by Hancock and Adams on the night of April 18, 1775. Given by Mrs. Asa Gray of Cambridge.

Old family Bible, cradle, big brass kettle, big iron pot, old-fashioned chair, sausage filler, mortar and pestle. From Mr. J. F. Simonds.

A push-plough used in early part of eighteenth century. A colored print of the Battle of Lexington (supposed to be one of the first pictures of the battle ever published), framed in old weather-beaten wood held together by wrought-iron nails, and mounted with a bayonet picked up on Dorchester Heights, supposed to have been left there by a Revolutionary soldier; also a book of ancient pictures of the Battle of Lexington and a sermon on the battle by Jonas Clarke. All from the late Mr. Charles A. Wellington.

A sermon on George Washington by Timothy Alden, Jr. From Mr. David W. Muzzey.

Two bound volumes of Boston daily newspapers, published immediately after the great fire in 1872, and the centennial celebration in 1875, from Mr. Geo. O. Smith.

xiv.   *GIFTS.*

A framed business card of Paul Revere. From Mr. C. A. Wellington.
A letter by Joseph Warren, written in the Provincial Congress, April 25, 1775.
A picture of the old Cradock house, Medford, Mass.; four dozen copies of description of the Battle of Lexington by Elias Phinney. All from estate of the late Mr. Charles A. Wellington.
A large framed photograph of the old Bowman house, the oldest house now standing in Lexington, built in 1649. From Mrs. Van Ness.
Platinum picture of Tidd house. From Mr. B. C. Whitcher.
Three chairs. From Misses F. M. and S. E. Robinson.
Feather bed, husk bed, cheese press, big three-gallon glass bottle, Dutch oven, implements used in the fur industry in Lexington, etc., from the Stephen Robbins homestead. Given by Miss Ellen A. Stone.
Pair of candle snuffers. From Mrs. W. F. Caldwell.
Jonathan Harrington's coffee mill. From Mrs. Harrison Pierce.
Vols. III., IV., V., VI., VII. of " Soldiers and Sailors of the Revolutionary War." From Commonwealth of Massachusetts.
Autograph copy of a page of Town Records of Fairfield, Conn., showing record of marriage of John Hancock and Dorothy Quincy, framed proclamation, many manuscripts, etc. From estate of Rev. E. G. Porter.
Desk said to have been used by Washington in Medford, and a hammock reel. From the Wellington estate.
Bullet mould, candle moulds, lamp filler, wooden crowbar, letter of Eliza Clarke to Mary Simonds, Lincoln presidential campaign papers. From estate of Mr. Joseph F. Simonds.
Iron shovel used in brick oven in Monument House, 1816. From Mrs. Sophia Davis.
Two volumes of Field genealogy. From Mr. Marshall Field, Chicago.
Several manuscripts, including Rev. A. B. Muzzey's " History of the Battle of Lexington." From Mr. Loring W. Muzzey.
A number of articles of historic interest, formerly owned by the late Charles A. Wellington. Presented by Mr. Cornelius Wellington.
Catalogue of Colburn collection of autographs and portraits in Bostonian Society. From Mr. D. H. Coolidge.
Pamphlet, " Two Colonial Dames, Dorothy Q. and Dorothy Quincy Hancock." From Colonial Dames of America, New York City.
Two pumpkin hoods, various articles of dress for a child, homespun

linen towel, two fancy vests and a teakettle. Partly donated and partly loaned by Miss Elizabeth Pierce.

Embroidered memorial mourning-piece, framed. From Miss Elvira W. Harrington.

Framed picture of William Dawes, Jr. From Miss Julia Goddard, Brookline.

Lamp and reflector formerly used in Universalist meeting-house, East Lexington; one large tray. Both from Miss Elizabeth Pierce.

Bedspread embroidered with figures from Hogarth's pictures. From Dr. J. O. Tilton.

Tassel from first chaise in Lexington. From Mr. Nathaniel Pierce.

Photograph of Dr. Seth Saltmarsh. From Miss Saltmarsh.

Cheese-curd basket. From Mr. A. Bradford Smith.

Old-time flail. From Mr. H. H. Tyler.

Dancing-boots worn by the late Nathaniel Pierce. From Miss Elizabeth Pierce.

Old-fashioned table. From Mrs. Oliver Brown.

Framed spray of arbor-vitae thrown by the Masons on the grave of Jonathan Harrington, last survivor of Battle of Lexington.

Antique bedspread made about 1770-1780, formerly owned by Daniel Brown of Boston, one of the Boston Tea Party. From Miss Elvira H. Brown, great-great-granddaughter of Daniel Brown.

Framed autograph letter from Hon. Robert C. Winthrop; four United States Philadelphia centennial medals. From Mrs. Everett S. Locke.

Bed and chairs. From Miss Elizabeth Pierce.

Vols. IX. and X., "Soldiers and Sailors of Revolutionary War." From Commonwealth of Massachusetts.

"Old Derry Field." From Manchester (N. H.) Hist. Society.

Etching of Munroe Tavern. From Mrs. James P. Munroe.

Sword, hat, canteen and knapsack, used by Josiah Harrington in Lexington Artillery Company. From Miss Lucy Harrington, Concord, Mass.

Suit of boy's clothes worn by Larkin Pierce when three years old, born 1798, died 1801. Given by Mrs. H. J. Nicoll and Mrs. H. B. Sampson.

Bits and bit braces used by David Tuttle about 1800.

Top of arch of welcome to Lafayette, painted on linen.

Moulding plane used in 1805. From Mr. D. A. Tuttle.

GIFTS.

Letters of Earl Percy, Vol. I. From Mr. C. K. Bolton, Boston Athenæum.

Two wooden candlesticks made from the Hancock elm after it was blown down. From Miss Cordelia Floyd, Waltham, Mass.

Horn snuffbox made about 1750 and used by Lucy, wife of Joseph Harrington. From Miss Lucy Harrington, Concord, Mass.

Hand loom. From Mr. George O. Smith.

Two pairs of shutters formerly on the Hancock-Clarke House. From Misses Rowena and Ellen L. Nash.

Paper and inscriptions in old cemetery. From Dr. Francis H. Brown.

Receipt of William Dimond, drummer of the minute men. From Mr. Samuel W. Child.

Large framed reprint of map made of Boston in 1722, and one showing the location of all property holders, streets, etc., in Lexington in 1853. From Mr. George O. Smith.

Manuscript record of deaths in Lexington from 1782 to 1854, kept by Jonathan Harrington. Given by Mrs. Harrison Pierce.

Old-fashioned brass snuffbox with 1745 engraved on the end. From Mr. George O. Smith.

Old warrant, in manuscript, of the town of Lexington in 1792.

Proceedings of Oneida Hist. Society of Utica, N. Y. From Mr. F. L. Proctor of Utica.

Drum beaten on Lexington Green, April 19, 1775, by William Dimond. From State of Massachusetts.

Fifteen valuable old pamphlets. From Mr. Edward T. Chandler.

Diplomatic coat worn by William Eustis when United States minister to the Court of The Hague. From estate of Mrs. George W. Porter.

Block design made in copper for printing calico. From Mr. A. D. Puffer.

Manuscript: Order for a General Court Martial to be held at Concord, 1788, addressed to Col. William Munroe of Lexington. Loaned by Mr. Frederick M. Munroe.

Pamphlet, " The Right to Bear Arms." From Mr. Henry S. Ruggles.

Valuable book published by the French Government, list of French soldiers and sailors in American Revolution. From the Secretary of State, U. S.

GIFTS.

Old volumes and sermons. From Mrs. T. E. Cutter.

Three medals conferred upon the late Baroness von Olnhausen by the German Emperor in recognition of her services as an army nurse. One of these medals, the Iron Cross, has been given to no other American except Clara Barton, head of the Red Cross Society. These medals were presented through Mr. James P. Munroe.

Letter seals owned by Theodore Parker. From Wellington family.

Card sent by Theodore Parker to Miss Caroline Thayer. From the Wellington family.

Sermons by Jonas Clarke and others. From Mr. Charles F. Greene, Saco, Me.

Framed picture of Amos Locke. From Mrs. G. F. Marvin, New York, and Miss Etta Locke, Lexington.

Iron skittle belonging to Harrington family. From Mrs. Otis Locke, Lynn.

Towel woven by Rebecca Mulliken before 1784. From Miss E. W. Harrington.

Paper on buildings erected by David Tuttle in Lexington. From Mr. D. A. Tuttle.

Confederate script, fifty cents. From Mr. Frank M. Alley.

Old-fashioned bonnet. From Mrs. Arthur W. Hamblen.

Piece of wood from Paul Revere pear-tree. From Canton, Mass.

Vols. XI. and XII. of "Massachusetts Soldiers and Sailors in Revolutionary War." From Massachusetts Secretary of State.

Files of auditors', school committee's and selectmen's reports. From Mrs. A. W. Hamblen.

Brick bearing the date 1647. From Mr. W. P. Hatch.

Brick taken from the cache at Pemaquid, Me. From Mr. George H. Cutter.

Pictures of house and bootshop of Warren Duren, Lexington; Park Street Church, Boston; Roger Williams house, Salem, two views; portraits of Abijah Harrington and wife; Brevet Major Sullivan Burbank and wife; address on "West Cambridge in 1775," by Samuel A. Smith, and a pamphlet entitled "A Plea." From Miss E. W. Harrington.

MEMBERSHIP.

HONORARY MEMBERS.

*Brown, G. Washington.
Clark, Miss Grace.
*Clark, Jonas B., Rev.
*Ellis, Geo. E., Rev. D. D.
Putnam, A. P., Rev. D. D.
Staples, Rev. Charles J.
*Winthrop, Robert C.

* Deceased.

LIFE MEMBERS.

Clapp, Robert P.
Whitcher, Miss Florence.

MEMBERS.

Ayer, Rev. and Mrs. J. C.
Bayley, Mr. and Mrs. E. A.
Batcheller, Mr. W. M.
Bennink, Mr. and Mrs. L. E.
Blinn, Miss Helen J.
Bliss, Mr. and Mrs. E. P.
Brown, Mr. and Mrs. B. F.
Brown, Mr. and Mrs. F. D.
Bryant, Mrs. Albert W.
Butler, Mr. William A.
Butters, Mrs. Frank V.
Butters, Miss S. L.
Carter, Rev. and Mrs. C. F.
Cary, Miss Alice B.
Childs, Mr. and Mrs. F. C.
Clapp, Mrs. R. P.
Cook, Miss Mabel P.
Carleton, Miss G. W.
Crosby, Mrs. Medora R.
Cutler, Mr. Alfred D.
Dale, Mr. and Mrs. Charles E.
Dana, Miss Ellen E.
Davis, Mr. and Mrs. C. B.
Davis, Mr. and Mrs. G. O
Dane, Mr. and Mrs. .F S.
Dean, Mr. and Mrs F. W.
Doe, Mr. and Mrs. C. C.
Fiske, Miss Carrie F.
Fiske, Miss Emma I.
Fobes, Mr. and Mrs. E. F.
Fowle, Mr. Charles A., Jr.
Fox, Mr. and Mrs. I. P.
Gilmore, Mr. and Mrs. G. L.
Goodwin, Mr. and Mrs. C. C.
Gookin, Mrs. Frances S.
Goulding, Mr. and Mrs. G. L.
Greeley, Mrs. H. M.
Hamlin, Miss Emma.
Harrington, Miss C. W.
Harrington, Miss E. E.
Harrington, Miss E. W.
Harrington, Miss Martha M.
Herrick, Mr. and Mrs. F. W.
Hudson, Miss Mary E.
Hunt, Miss Anstiss S.
Hunt, Mrs. E. M.
Hitchcock, Mr. and Mrs. W. A.
Hunt, Mr. and Mrs. William.
Hutchinson, Mrs. J. F.
Kirkland, Miss Marian P.
Kettell, Mr. and Mrs. C. W.
Knowlton, Mr. Clarence H.
Lane, Mrs. Ellen B.
Lane, Mr. Ralph E.

MEMBERSHIP.

Locke, Mr. and Mrs. A. E.
Locke, Miss Etta M.
Locke, Mr. and Mrs. H. G.
Locke, Hon. Warren E.
Luke, Mr. and Mrs. W. J.
Merriam, Mr. E. P.
Milne, Mr. and Mrs. G. D.
Mitchell, Mr. A. S.
Mulliken, Miss Amelia M.
Mulliken, Mr. E. M.
Munroe, Miss M. Alice.
Munroe, Miss Elmina.
Munroe, Mr. Howard M.
Munroe, Mrs. Helen H.
Munroe, Mr. and Mrs. J. P.
Munroe, Mr. James S.
Nichols, Mr. E. P.
Nunn, Mr. Charles P.
Parker, Mr. Charles M.
Parker, Miss Elizabeth S.
Parsons, Mr. and Mrs. A. S.
Peaslee, Mrs. Louise W.
Perkins, Mr. and Mrs. Walter B.
Phinney, Miss Jane.
Pierce, Mr. Alfred
Pierce, Mr. and Mrs. C. F.
Pierce, Miss Gertrude.
Piper, Dr. Fred S.
Putnam, Mr. and Mrs. H. H.
Porter, Mr. and Mrs. H. W.
Raymond, Mrs. F. F.
Raymond, Mr. Henry S.
Redman, Mrs A. M.
Reed, Mr. and Mrs. Hammon.
Robertson, Miss Emma A.
Robinson, Miss Frances M.
Robinson, Mrs. F. O.
Robinson, Miss Sarah E.
Robinson, Mr. and Mrs. Theo. P.
Russell, Mr. and Mrs. J. F.
Rowse, Mr. and Mrs. W. W.
Saville, Mr. L. A.

Scott, Hon. and Mrs. A. E.
Seeley, Mr. and Mrs. O. G.
Shaw, Mr. Elijah A.
Shaw, Miss Elsie L.
Smith, Mr. A. Bradford.
Smith, Miss Charlotte E.
Sherburne, Mr. and Mrs. F. F.
Sherburne, Mr. and Mrs. Warren.
Skerry, Miss Sarah R.
Spaulding, Mr. and Mrs. G. W.
Staples, Mrs. C. A.
Stevens, Mr. and Mrs. R. L.
Stevens, Rev. and Mrs. A. W.
Streeter, Mr. and Mrs. G. H.
Stickle, Mr. and Mrs. W. C.
Stone, Mr. Edward C.
Taylor, Mr. Edward G.
Taylor, Mr. and Mrs. George W.
Tenney, Mrs. Benjamin F.
Thornton, Mrs. Annie C.
Thornton, Miss Mary C.
Thornton, Miss Elizabeth T.
Tilton, Dr. J. O.
Tower, Mrs. William A.
Tower, Miss Ellen M.
Valentine, Dr. and Mrs. Henry C.
Van Ness, Mrs. Sarah B.
Washburn, Mr. and Mrs. A. W.
Wellington, Miss Caroline.
Wellington, Mr. Cornelius.
Wellington, Miss Eliza.
Wellington, Mr. Herbert L.
Wellington, Mr. Walter.
Wetherbee, Mr. and Mrs. A. A.
Whiting, Mr. and Mrs. G. O.
Whitman, Miss Kate.
Willard, Mr. and Mrs. J. H.
Wiswell, Mr. and Mrs. C. H.
Wood, Mrs. Adelaide H.
Worthen, Mr. George E.
Wright, Miss Abbie E.
Wright, Miss Emma E.

NECROLOGY.

Alderman, Franklin,	February 9, 1900
Babcock, Leonard G.,	March 14, 1900
Bowman, Mrs. Eliza Powell,	June 12, 1899
Bryant, Albert W.,	November 21, 1902
Chandler, John Q. A.,	December 14, 1896
Clarke, Mrs. Ruth B.,	June 29, 1889
Davis, Mrs. Mary A. E.,	March 3, 1890
Gammell, Miss Lucy,	December 22, 1889
Gookin, Samuel H.,	September 23, 1894
Gould, Arthur F.,	October 6, 1890
Greeley, William H.,	December 21, 1889
Ham, James N.,	
Hamlin, Dr. Cyrus,	August 3, 1900
Harrington, Mrs. Miriam A.,	July 29, 1896
Hastings, John,	April 20, 1895
Hayes, Francis B.,	September 20, 1884
Hayes, Mrs. Margaret M.,	November 20, 1890
Hunt, Lewis,	November 29, 1893
Hutchinson, Mrs. Mary L.,	August 22, 1893
Jones, George F.,	June 2, 1898
Locke, Amos,	June 6, 1898
Lord, Mrs. Kate E.,	September 19, 1895
Meredith, Rev. Irving,	May 8, 1894
Merriam, Mrs. Jane,	December 31, 1895
Merriam, Hon. Matthew H.,	January 26, 1898
Matthews, Capt. Richard,	December 11, 1893
Mills, Henry F.,	1898
Mulliken, Emory A.,	September 5, 1899
Mulliken, William H.,	November 19, 1889
Munroe, Mrs. Alice B.,	August 7, 1888
Munroe, William H.,	August 28, 1902
Munroe, William R.,	September 6, 1889
Munroe, Henry A.,	June 18, 1896
Muzzey, George E.,	December 14, 1896
Paine, Francis B.,	
Paine, George A.,	1889
Parker, James,	March 22, 1890

Parker, Miss Esther T.,	March 8, 1898
Parker, Theo. J.,	June 20, 1892
Perkins, Dr. W. O.,	
Pierce, Mrs. Etta A.,	December 26, 1896
Pitts, Mrs. Meta Wilson,	January 26, 1897
Porter, Rev. Edward G.,	February 5, 1900
Porter, D. D., Rev. George W.,	March 2, 1896
Powers, Jacob Haven,	September 15, 1899
Putnam, Mrs. E. A.,	January 23, 1890
Redman, Mrs. Emma S.,	December 27, 1898
Reed, Henry M.,	June 27, 1895
Richardson, Herbert E.,	
Robinson, Frederick O.,	February 1, 1905
Robinson, George W.,	December 16, 1893
Sampson, Grace D.,	February 6, 1902
Saltmarsh, Dr. Seth,	February 8, 1897
Saville, Mrs. Rebecca H.,	June 27, 1894
Simonds, Eli,	
Simonds, Joseph F.,	September 17, 1897
Smith, Mrs. Caroline T.,	December 26, 1894
Smith, George O.,	November 16, 1903.
Smith, William H.,	September 24, 1893
Stackpole, Charles A.,	December 16, 1890
Staples, Rev. Carlton A.,	August 30, 1904
Stone, Mrs. Alice A.,	September 23, 1898
Stone, Mrs. Ellen A.,	October 28, 1890
Sumner, Mrs. Maria,	November 29, 1898
Tilton, Mrs. Harriett A.,	October 24, 1887
Thornton, Col. Charles C. G.,	January 13, 1898
Todd, Nathaniel M.,	April 25, 1900
Tower, Col. William A.,	November 21, 1904
Tyler, Mrs. Mary E.,	April 7, 1897
Viles, Miss Rebecca D.,	April 23, 1893
Wellington, Mrs. Caroline B.,	June 1, 1892
Wellington, Charles A.,	February 2, 1901
Wellington, Horatio,	
Willis, Frank R.,	April 13, 1891
Wright, Luke W.,	April 22, 1888
Wyman, Mrs. A. Theresa,	December 4, 1898

INDEX.

	PAGE.
Adams, Samuel, Statue of,	68
Alexander, Miss Frances,	38
Anti-Slavery Society,	48, 51
Banns, Publishing the,	91
Baptist Society,	39
Barrett, Rev. Fiske,	39
Bay State Historical League,	169
Beacon Hill,	9
Brattle Street Church,	9
Briggs, Rev. Charles,	37, 87, 90
Brown, Francis,	82
Brown, Dr. F. H.,	95
Brown, Deacon James,	91
Bryant, Albert W.,	142
Buckman Tavern,	94, 103, 143
Buckminster, Rev. J. S.,	9
Cambridge Farms,	25, 98, 143
Carter, Rev. C. F.,	177
Cary, Miss A. B.,	140
Centennial, Lexington,	62
Chandler, E. F.,	127
Chandler, S. E.,	127
Channing, Rev. W. E.,	47, 54, 57
Charles River Bridge,	110
Chittendon and Burr,	137
Clapp, R. P.,	169, 173
Clarke, Rev. Jonas,	16, 32, 40, 87, 98, 102, 140, 146
Clock-making,	134
Concord Turnpike,	110
Currier, Dr. W. J.,	22
Dow, G. W.,	122
Emerson, R. W.,	50
Epitaphs, Lexington,	94

INDEX.

	PAGE
Estabrook, Benjamin,	27, 28, 37
Faneuil, Peter,	11, 13
Fisk, Dr. Joseph,	19
Flip,	154
Follen, Rev. Charles,	42
Follen Church,	38, 50, 52
Follen, Mrs. Eliza Lee,	47, 54
Gannett, Rev. E. S.,	37
Garrison, W. L.,	48, 51, 57
German Student Corps,	43
Gerrish, Samuel,	8
Grant, President U. S.,	75
Green, Mrs. C. M.,	140
Hancock-Clarke House,	7, 14, 30, 138, 146, 162, 179
Hancock, Rev. Ebenezer,	7, 14, 30, 31, 40
Hancock, Rev. John,	7, 14, 29, 40
Hancock, Hon. John,	14, 17, 34, 68, 86
Hancock, Mrs. Lydia (Henchman),	8, 18, 33
Hancock Mansion,	10
Hancock, Thomas,	5, 30
Harrington, Miss E. W.,	134
Harrington, Jonathan,	100
Hastings, Deacon Isaac,	91
Hayes Fountain,	163
Healy, G. P. A.,	22
Herlackenden, Roger,	98
High School, Lexington,	117
Hiram Lodge of Masons,	142, 148
Historical Relics,	65
Hogarth's "Apprentices,"	5
Holmes, Miss S. E.,	97
"Holy Alliance," The,	45
Hudson, Charles,	134
Hudson, Miss M. E.,	62, 117
Jones, Paul,	77
Lafayette,	46
Lane, R. E.,	19
Lexington & West Cambridge R. R.,	58
Lexington, Battle of,	34, 101, 146
Lexington, Town of,	30, 37

	PAGE
"Lexington," Burning of the, .	. 55
Livermore, Rev. L. J., . .	40
Martineau, Harriet, . . .	. . 51
Meeting Houses, Lexington, .	. 27, 82
Middlesex Canal, ...	. 110
Minute Men of 1875,	. . 64
Mulliken Clocks, .	134
Mulliken, John, . .	135
Mulliken, Nathaniel, .	 134
Munroe, J. P., . .	12, 159, 169, 182
Munroe, John, . .	. . . 99
Munroe, Jonas, . .	. . 149
Munroe, William,	100, 143
Munroe Tavern,	142
Muzzey, G. E., . .	139
New England Historic-Genealogical Society, . . .	. 96
Parker, Capt. John, ...	. 102
Parker, Rev. Theodore, ...	42, 115
Parsons, A. S., ...	. . 160
Pelham, Herbert, ... 142	25, 98, 142
Phillips, Wendell, ...	. . 53
Pitcairn Pistols, . . .	. . 66
Porter, Rev. E. G.,	64, 178
Putnam, Mrs. J. P.,	. . 66
Quincy, Dorothy, . .	. . . 18
Revere, Paul, ...	. . 146
Robbins Burying Ground.	. 101
Robbins, Eli M., ...	96, 100
Robbins, Thomas, ...	. 102
Russell, Hon. James, ...	. 59
Scott, Hon. A. E., ...	155
Simonds, Joshua, ...	102
Singing Schools, ...	36, 84
Smith, A. Bradford, ...	110
Smith, George O., ...	158, 164
Smith, G. O., Will of, ...	165, 174
Spaulding, Dr. Stillman, . . .	19, 37
Stafford, Miss, ...	76
Staples, Rev. C. A., ... 5, 25, 40, 97, 138, 155, 102, 164, 177, 182
Staples, Rev. N. A., ... 39

INDEX.

	PAGE
Stone, Capt. John,	110
Swett, Rev. W. G.,	38
Town Meetings,	32, 118, 130
Walker, Rev. James,	37
Warren, W. W.,	58
Washington, President,	153
Wellington, Benjamin,	102
Wellington, Charles A.,	155
Wellington, George Y.,	58
Wellington, Jeduthan,	114
Wellington, Dr. Timothy,	59
West Cambridge,	58, 150
Westcott, Rev. Henry,	40
Whitman, Rev. Jason,	39
Whitman, Dr. M. F.,	132
Whittemore, H. O.,	131
Williams, Rev. Avery,	36, 87, 89

www.ingramcontent.com/pod-product-compliance
Lightning Source LLC
Chambersburg PA
CBHW031818220426
43662CB00007B/705